High Attention Reading

High Attention Reading

Preparing Students for Independent Reading of Informational Text

Elizabeth Hale

TEACHERS COLLEGE PRESS

TEACHERS COLLEGE | COLUMBIA UNIVERSITY
NEW YORK AND LONDON

Published by Teachers College Press,® 1234 Amsterdam Avenue, New York, NY 10027

Front cover by Rebecca Lown Design. Photo of children by wavebreakmedia. Photo of books by Alexey t17. Both images via Shutterstock.

Library of Congress Cataloging-in-Publication Data

Names: Hale, Elizabeth, 1971– author.
Title: High attention reading : preparing students for independent reading of informational text / Elizabeth Hale.
Description: New York, NY : Teachers College Press, [2022] | Includes bibliographical references and index.
Identifiers: LCCN 2022027153 (print) | LCCN 2022027154 (ebook) | ISBN 9780807767290 (hardcover) | ISBN 9780807767283 (paperback) | ISBN 9780807781197 (ebook)
Subjects: LCSH: Reading. | Reading comprehension. | Children—Books and reading.
Classification: LCC LB1050 .H264 2022 (print) | LCC LB1050 (ebook) | DDC 372.47—dc23/eng/20220810
LC record available at https://lccn.loc.gov/2022027153
LC ebook record available at https://lccn.loc.gov/2022027154

ISBN 978-0-8077-6728-3 (paper)
ISBN 978-0-8077-6729-0 (hardcover)
ISBN 978-0-8077-8119-7 (ebook)

Printed on acid-free paper
Manufactured in the United States of America

This book is dedicated to
Xavier L. Rozas
My partner in life and love

Contents

Acknowledgments

Thank you to the many teachers who made HART come alive in their classrooms, especially Michelle Decerbo, Pam Pitts and Michelle Gulla from Boston Public Schools, and Lisa Weinstock and Erica Miller from Framingham Public Schools, who were all there in the beginning. A huge thank you to all the teachers and staff at Tiger Academy in Jacksonville, especially Steve Jolly, Edward Moore, Tonia Fuller, Rodina Hughes, Charles McWhite and Lauren Gibbs, for welcoming me into the Tiger family and for bringing HART into classrooms. A shout out to all the 4th and 5th grade scholars at Tiger Academy—you are simply the best!

A huge thank you to my academic family at the University of North Florida. I feel incredibly lucky that my path led me to a college of education with such supportive and caring faculty and staff. A special thanks to John White, my partner in the Seven Bridges Writing Project and the mission to bring engagement back into the forefront of reading and writing. Thank you also to Diane Yendol-Hoppey for your incredible leadership. Also thank you to Katrina Hall, Pam Williamson, Lunetta Williams, Georgia Miller, Paul Parkison, Becci Burns, and Bess Wilson for your friendship and support, and to Dan Dinsmore for your ongoing support and advice. I am also grateful to have connected with Rob Kelly and Fay Blake of Read USA and found a partner in bringing book choice and reading engagement alive for children. Thank you to Emily Spangler at Teachers College Press for connecting with me on this topic years ago and your guidance in this process.

Finally thank you to my always there, always supportive family: my parents, Stan and Sandy Hale, and my twin sister, Christine Landino. To my own children, Dexter, Emma and Leo, you are the brightest lights in my life.

Introduction
Why Have HART

I remember the exact day I realized something different was needed when it came to students' independent reading of informational text. I was working as a literacy coach with a 5th-grade teacher in Boston Public Schools, and we were in the middle of a nonfiction unit of study. At first, we were so pleased at the start of the unit as we looked around the room during independent reading. Students were sitting in various places, bean bags in the rug area, some on fold out beach chairs here and there, all quietly reading the nonfiction books they had picked out to read as soft classical music played in the background. Then we each went to check in on some of the students. First, I went over to Dante. Just the top of his head was visible, the rest hidden behind a big, blue hard cover book with a large shark on the front.

"Dante, how's that book?" I asked. Dante poked his head up with surprised eyes and then smiled.

"Good! They're scary but I keep wanting to read about them," to which I laughed and said I could relate. When I asked him what he was learning, he pointed to the picture.

"See this one? Look at his teeth! He could totally bite off my arm!" he said with mock horror. Dante then proceeded to talk about the sharks in the pictures, flipping back to pages he already read. The more I asked about what he learned, the more I wondered if he had been reading much of the text at all. When I asked, he readily admitted that he did read some of the words "a little bit" but mostly looked at the pictures and read the captions under the photographs of sharks.

As I stood up and said good-bye to Dante, I realized I had been making assumptions about his reading based on how he looked. He seemed so *engaged* in his reading. And in a sense, he was. Many educators understand the importance of encouraging and even teaching students to garner information from the text features that fill many of today's informational texts such as captions, photographs, and diagrams (Harvey & Goudvis, 2007). On another day I might have reminded myself of that and moved on to the next student. But instead, on that day, I thought about the 6th-grade class I had just visited the day before at a nearby K–8 Boston Public school where taller versions of these students were pulling textbooks out of their lockers and getting homework that largely comprised of content area reading. The reading they did throughout the day, and were assigned for homework that night, reflected the reality that the majority of texts students read once they reach middle and high school grades is informational and that almost all of it is done independently (Moss, 2005).

Suddenly, with these two adjacent grades fresh in my mind, I saw a huge gap. But it was not about the presence of informational text. In previous decades, there had been a visible increase in discussions at the district level about informational texts propelled by research that emphasized the need to increase elementary students' exposure to and experience with informational texts at an early age (Duke, 2004; Maloch & Bomer, 2013; Moss, 2015; Yopp & Yopp, 2012), a sentiment echoed by the Common Core State Standards (National Governors Association Center for Best Practices, 2010). I also personally saw increases in the number of informational texts that were used as read-alouds or in guided reading by teachers, fueled by publishing companies that had, fortunately, responded to the same research.

The gap I saw that day was not about the number of nonfiction books in classrooms but about the amount of time our students were spending reading informational texts independently and, as illustrated by Dante, how they were doing that reading. Putting more nonfiction books in the hands of elementary students is important, but not enough. If we are to really prepare students for the demands of middle and high school reading, then there has to be a scaffolding toward these expectations. While I have seen lots of lessons and programs that are designed to scaffold knowledge of informational text as a genre or critical and higher-order thinking skills during or after reading, what I have not seen is scaffolding around what most impacts the quality of independent reading with informational text: the *effort* of attending to text. As Elfrieda Hiebert (2014) points out, lack of proficiency in reading achievement is often not due to students' inability to read, rather "what many cannot do is independently maintain reading focus over long periods of time. The proficiency they lack is stamina—the ability to sustain mental effort without the scaffolds or adult support" (p. 2).

Concern about preparation for the particular area of independent reading of informational text is also echoed in the common core state standards:

> There is also evidence that current standards, curriculum, and instructional practice have not done enough to foster the independent reading of complex texts so crucial for college and career readiness, particularly in the case of informational texts. . . . Current trends suggest that if students cannot read challenging texts with understanding—if they have not developed the skill, concentration, and stamina to read such texts—they will read less in general. In particular, if students cannot read complex expository text to gain information, they will likely turn to text-free or text-light sources, such as video, podcasts, and tweets. These sources, while not without value, cannot capture the nuance,

subtlety, depth, or breadth of ideas developed through complex text. (National Governors Association Center For Best Practices, 2010, Appendix A, p. 3)

INFORMATIONAL TEXTS VERSUS STORIES

There are many reasons why independent reading of informational text requires a different skill than reading stories. Informational texts tend to be more lexically dense than stories and contain more content-specific vocabulary and academic language (Gardner, 2004; Hirsch, 2003; Snow, 2002). In addition, most informational texts rarely follow the familiar arc of a story the way a biography might, which provides an important schema for new information (Best et al., 2008). Also, unlike stories, informational texts tend to be more abstract in nature with content that is often removed from children's everyday experiences (Graesser et al., 2003). Combined, these characteristics simply place more demands on a reader to sustain continued attention and comprehension.

These differences between reading information and stories, of course, are not unique to children. I have been highly motivated when reading many informational texts. One example from my own experience is *The Professor Is In* by Karen Kelsky (2015), a book about academic job searches that is now full of blue underlines and notes in the margins from when I was applying for academic positions, reflecting my desire to learn all I could from those pages. As motivated as I was while reading this book, that experience was nothing like another book I was reading around the same time called *The Nightingale* by Kristen Hannah (2015). Both books are well written. But reading *The Nightingale* was like being carried away on a river: once I would get back to the book, I literally feel swept away by the story. When you find a truly great author, the experience is effortless. Returning to that book felt like getting back to a movie on demand and pressing play. No matter how well written the academic job search book was or how motivated I was to learn information embedded in those words, reading *The Professor Is In* would never be quite the same as reading my novel. And it is not supposed to be: genre differences exist for a reason. The different types of texts reflect the different purposes of why we open up each type of book.

As educators we want students to grow up to appreciate, be skilled at, and enjoy reading both genres. And both types of texts require a myriad of skills that schools teach from phonics, fluency and strategies for decoding unknown words to thinking critically about what we read. But the ability to read informational text well is arguably the gatekeeper of academic success in school. The earlier we can help students to independently read, not just more informational texts, but to read those texts with intention and stamina, the better. These qualities, importantly, not only support greater literal and inferential comprehension but also greater engagement with and motivation to read this genre.

HIGH ATTENTION READING THROUGH TALKING

The purpose of this book is to describe a reading format called High Attention Reading through Talking (HART) that was designed for this very purpose: to scaffold the habits of mind behind high quality independent reading of informational text while also exposing students to a wide range of science and social studies topics. The main driver of this format is the use of small, student-driven groups that alternate between short segments of independent reading and discussion in order to impact accountability and motivation to read text with more attention and effort than they would on their own. In essence, HART targets the internal process of reading, both from a cognitive and affective standpoint, with the goal of improving not just the quantity of informational text students read but the quality of that reading.

To be clear, the idea of supporting students to be attentive and aware of comprehension is not new. Many teachers and reading programs, including those specific to science literacy, emphasize the importance of modeling and teaching metacognitive strategies that target attending to comprehension (Avargil et al., 2018; Pressley, 2001). Such strategies, however, tend to favor the more motivated readers, since using them independently requires intention on the part of the reader in the first place. The purpose of HART is not to replace instruction of metacognitive skills such as monitoring comprehension or to diminish their value, but to *expand* teachers' toolboxes for influencing the specific and critically important but often hard-to-reach space of students' internal habits of mind when they read silently, and to do so for all students, especially those who are not already motivated readers.

Since there is more to preparing students to independently read informational text than just attending as one reads, HART is designed to scaffold additional aspects of reading this genre, including book choice, activating background knowledge, attending to vocabulary, and thinking critically about what one learns through writing. Table 0.1 illustrates the different components of HART and the specific aspects of reading each one supports.

Table 0.1. Components of HART

HART Component	Scaffolding for
Choosing Sets of Books	Book Choice
What Do You Know?	Background Knowledge
Word Quiz	Content-Specific Vocabulary
Read and Share	Engagement and Comprehension
Reader's Notebook	Critical Thinking About Texts

Figure 0.1. A Model of Pearson and Gallagher's (1983) Gradual Release of Responsibility

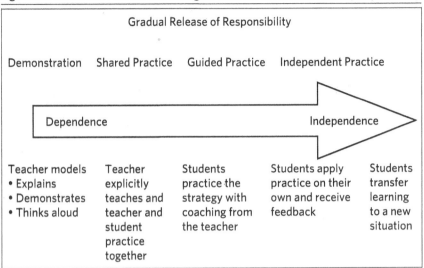

The idea of scaffolding these literacy concepts is also not new. Talking about one's background knowledge about a topic or content vocabulary, for example, is often modeled in read-alouds and explicitly taught and supported in small-group instruction such as guided reading. But HART occupies an important and not always represented space in the gradual release of responsibility continuum (Pearson & Gallagher, 1983), shown in Figure 0.1. Most classroom scaffolding for reading, regardless of whether it is preplanned or contingent, falls squarely under guided practice, where "students practice the strategy with coaching from the teacher."

Far less prevalent is that critical space in between guided practice and independence where "students apply practice on their own and receive feedback." Therefore, while some readings strategies that students practice in HART are widely taught and practiced, what students have typically not yet experienced is self-initiating these strategies. Not only does this heightened independence impact engagement because it aligns with students' growing desire for autonomy as they move toward and into middle and high school (Eccles et al., 1993), but by placing more ownership on the students, there is a greater likelihood of transfer when they are completely independent.

HOW HART DIFFERS FROM OTHER READING FORMATS

The student-run aspect of HART is similar to the ownership exhibited by literature circles, a format in which small groups of students gather together to have in-depth and student-facilitated discussions about what they read

(Daniels, 2002) as well as other discussion formats such as Questioning the Author (Beck et al., 1997). In much the same way these student-centered discussion formats reflect the important penultimate space in the gradual release continuum in regard to thinking critically about texts, HART reflects this next-to-last step in regard to quality independent reading of informational texts.

While all of these formats are meant to foster engagement in reading, there are important differences between the purpose of literature circles and HART. First, while literature circles can include both novels and nonfiction texts, HART has an explicit focus on the wide reading of informational texts. The primary difference, however, is how discussion is used in each format. In literature circles, discussion is primarily used as a vehicle for engaging students in critical thinking about what they read (Daniels, 2002). In HART, the social and interactive aspect of student-to-student discussion is also used to encourage students to process and think about what they read but the talk is also designed to create high attention engaged reading because it creates a sense of accountability while students are reading independently. HART discussions take place in short intermittent periods of time that alternate with independent reading. The purpose of discussion is less about stimulating in-depth, extended conversation after reading and more about affecting the level of engagement that occurs while students are reading.

The fact that HART has little explicit naming or teaching of critical thinking skills, such as predicting or inferring, belies the fact that it encourages these important skills. Rather than focus on the teaching of these comprehension skills to engender high-quality reading, HART attends to the other side of this relationship. That is, it gets students to read in a high-quality way, driven by authentic, peer-driven accountability and coupled with achievable, short-term tasks, which then promotes the use of comprehension skills while reading. This type of reading, which is more likely to encourage the use of comprehension skills *while* reading, also provides an important foundation for subsequent critical thinking. There is no better preparation for the thinking that students do in their reader's notebook, or in a literature discussion, than students taking in what they read to the best of their ability. Additionally, the talk that students do in HART, while it might initially focus on literal comprehension of text, is meant to and can easily be elevated so that students are pushed to bring different types and levels of thinking into this conversational space. As will be explored later in this book, once students know how to do HART on their own, there is an intentional focus on students incorporating critical thinking into their discussions as well as into the writing they do in reader's notebooks.

Another aspect that is unique to HART compared to other discussion-focused reading formats is that it is meant to scaffold and be a temporary substitute for independent reading, at least with informational texts. Whereas most other discussion formats are meant to be done after students finish independent reading, discussion in HART is part of the independent reading experience. Therefore, while critical thinking can be brought into the talk students do in HART, teachers can also pair HART with other instructional formats that focus on longer, more involved discussions of text.

While HART is meant to be a whole-class format, meaning all students are doing HART at the same time, it is highly differentiated. Each group of students is reading texts matched to their appropriate reading level so that all students can access texts, a concept that is particularly important and beneficial for students who are below–grade-level readers. Students also choose books based on interest. Although there is structured choice, that is, students choose from sets of books on their level, HART libraries are meant to contain a range of levels about similar scientific and social studies topics. Throughout the book are descriptions of how HART can also be differentiated specifically for English learners.

HART was originally designed to target the upper elementary grades in order to prepare students for middle school reading, but it can be used by teachers of any grade including those at the middle and high school level. Because this format focuses on content area reading, it can be used by science and social studies teachers in addition to elementary and English Language Arts teachers who are looking for a way to support wide reading and build students' background knowledge in a way that complements direct instruction. HART can also be used as part of after-school programs to increase both the quantity and quality of reading students do with informational texts in a way that is structured but also engaging. The last chapter of this book also describes a primary version of HART called HART Junior that uses informational read-alouds and is designed for beginning readers.

ORGANIZATION OF THIS BOOK

The next chapter gives an overview of the different components of HART and discusses the logistics of getting started, including grouping students, organizing texts, and teaching HART book choice to students. Chapter 2 describes the first prereading step in HART called "What Do You Know?" which supports student ownership in thinking about background knowledge of a topic. This chapter also introduces the topic of scaffolding and how the design of HART (even while the skills themselves may not be new for teachers or students) takes students further along the gradual release of responsibility to allow for greater autonomy and ownership compared to small-group instruction formats. Chapter 3 describes the next prereading component called Word Quiz, which promotes attention to and discussion of content vocabulary. Chapter 4 describes the main part of HART, which is when students alternate between independent reading and student-driven conversation. Included in this chapter are discussions about why this format, that is the inclusion of talk *within* independent reading, is so instrumental to impacting students' attention and effort while reading.

Chapter 5 moves from the format of HART itself to how teachers can elevate the critical thinking that students do, both during HART discussions and with reader's notebooks. Chapter 6 is dedicated to assessment and responsive instruction in relation to HART. This chapter offers guidance on how teachers can formally assess HART and provide formative feedback through minilessons and group conferences. In the Appendices are lesson plans for teaching HART as well as copiables of any supportive documents. Chapter 7 offers suggestions of how HART can be incorporated into a school week or year and how HART can be altered for the primary grades and for middle and high school teachers using textbooks. This final chapter also takes a big-picture view of content-area reading and why it matters so much from both a curricular and social justice perspective.

CHAPTER 1

Getting Started

An important characteristic of HART is that it is not a reading program or curriculum: it is simply a way for students to do independent reading in a scaffolded context. This means that if independent reading is already part of your schedule (and hopefully it is!), then HART is not something you do in *addition* to independent reading. You might use HART as part of a nonfiction unit of study for several months to lift up the way students read this genre before returning to the more typical independent reading. Or you might choose to do HART two or three times a week all year long and have the more traditional independent reading on the other days. Regardless of how you use HART, there are elements that are different enough from regular independent reading that it requires specific materials as well as instruction about the different components so that students can facilitate the small-group conversations on their own.

GROUPING STUDENTS

HART teams are ideally made up of three or four students. This size is big enough to have collaborative conversations and still have a group should a student be absent, but not so big that a less vocal student can get lost in the group. Reading levels as determined by fall assessments and running records should be the primary factor in determining who is in which group. Some students in a group may not be at the exact same level as others, which is fine. Grouping is not as detailed as putting the 4.2s together and the 4.6s together, but rather looking for students who generally read at a 4th-grade level, regardless of what grade they are in. There is bound to be a variety of reading abilities in some groups, but what matters most is that no student is reading a text at a frustration level.

Although there are arguments for students at any grade level being exposed to and reading grade-level–content texts, the very goals of HART necessitate that every student can access and comprehend most of what they are reading independently. There is also an argument for having times during the week for heterogenous groups, when students of different ability levels are grouped together. A common perception about grouping students, however, is

Figure 1.1. Students Talking in a HART Team

that mixing students of different levels will always benefit lower-performing students by exposing them to more critical thinking and vocabulary. The flip side of being exposed to more elaborate explanations and reasoning of higher-ability peers is that social interactions in these groups can take on more of a student–teacher relationship, creating a situation where lower ability students tend to be on the receiving end of explanations (Murphy et al., 2017). There are even studies that have found low-ability students in homogenous groups were actually more engaged in conversation and co-constructing of knowledge (Lou et al., 1996; Murphy et al., 2017).

This similar ability grouping by level, then, is not done by default. One of the most important aspects of HART is that students talk about what they learned with someone else who is reading the same text. Sharing learning in any fashion is a positive task, but there is a crucial accountability factor at play when the person next to you just read the same exact book with the same sentences and vocabulary. This authentic peer accountability is what creates not just engaged talk but engaged independent reading, a concept that will be explored further in a later chapter.

For the many classrooms that have English learners (ELs), students' reading level in English should still determine groupings. Ideally nonnative English speakers are not all placed in the same group but rather dispersed throughout groups, which can offer additional support for both receptive and expressive content vocabulary. This suggestion rests on the purpose of the small groups in HART. If content learning, rather than reading and speaking, was the primary goal of HART, then it might make sense to place students in L1 groups where they can use their native language to express more complex ideas (Rance-Roney, 2010). Although students' development of science and social studies background knowledge is absolutely a key benefit and purpose of HART, the primary purpose is supporting the internal, fluent reading of texts in the academic language of school. For teachers in bilingual schools, of course, where students learn and process content in two languages throughout the day, the target language of school may be English or a different language, or a combination of both.

SELECTING TEXT SETS

The texts you provide for HART will, of course, depend on the resources available in your school and classroom. Sets of informational texts made for guided reading work well. Each set typically comes with four to six books, which gives a little cushion room for a lost book. More importantly, these books published just for reading in school are made to be high-interest about a range of topics with numerous text features, including colorful photographs and diagrams and come in a wide range of levels. Teachers needing to supplement their HART library with levels outside their grade range can consult teachers in other grades for sets of books to borrow.

Since HART is meant to support development of background knowledge, I highly recommend choosing sets of books that reflect not just a single topic but the network of knowledge that surrounds a topic. Content knowledge, after all, occurs not in learning about one single topic but in developing a schema of interrelated sets of information or concept networks (Fitzgerald et al., 2017). Understanding the life cycle of a frog, for example, is inherently connected with our understanding of freshwater habitats versus saltwater, breathing characteristics of amphibians, and concepts of metamorphosis. Each one of these concepts has their own knowledge network. Understanding breathing characteristics of amphibians, for example, relates to knowledge of oxygen and carbon dioxide, the structures of lungs versus gills, and even the properties of skin. There are also topics that perhaps are not central to one's understanding of frogs, but are enhanced by this knowledge. A student who is reading about deforestation, for example, is more likely to better comprehend sections that describe the impact to swamplands if they have previously read about frogs and their habitats, but it also makes this information more meaningful.

Figure 1.2 shows sets of books from one of the portable HART bins created by Read USA for their after-school program, that reflects networks of knowledge related to the water cycle. Each photograph shows the different sets students can choose from at each level. You will notice that while the 3rd-grade level books may be mostly different than the 2nd- and 4th-grade level books, they all represent concepts that relate to water. Our understanding

Figure 1.2. HART Book Sets by Level

of water pollution, for example, both supports and is enhanced by our understanding of the actual water cycle. So too is our understanding of rainfall deepened by and deepens our understanding of the water cycle itself. The addition of *Snowflake Bentley* (Martin & Azarian, 1998), a biography about Wilson Bentley who first photographed snowflakes and discovered what is now common knowledge that no two snowflakes are alike, is a great example of a book that may be several degrees removed from the concept of the water cycle, but offers a wonderfully rich contribution to network knowledge around water. Consider this one line from the book: "Of all the forms of water the tiny six-pointed crystals of ice called snow are incomparably the most beautiful and varied." Not only does a variety of texts and genre related to a central content topic support and reflect how knowledge is actually developed, but this variety is just more interesting and engaging for students compared to say, four separate books about the water cycle.

Sets of informational texts should be organized in bins by general science and social studies topics such as space, the human body, government, or countries. The categories should be general enough that you can stock them with at least three or four sets of books that reflect the different reading levels of your students. Each set can be kept together with a rubber band and should have a colored dot or some other symbol indicating the level. Another way to organize HART books is to have a portable bin, in which sets of books are kept in hanging folders that are the same color as the leveled dots. A benefit of these closed bins is that they can be kept in shelves but not take up space in your regular classroom library. These books are also less likely to become disorganized or go missing.

The portable and storable bins are particularly useful for the context of an after-school program where teachers are not in their own classrooms. This portable feature also allows for movement. With Read USA, for example, one school in Jacksonville currently has the "Water" and "Light & Energy" bins, while another school has the bins about "Animals and Sea Life" and "Planets and the Solar System." After four weeks, there is a coordinated exchange of bins so students have new topics to read during HART. This exchange system, which in this case is between schools within a district, could also be used between different classrooms within a school. While this system requires collaboration and communication, it is a way to keep costs down for each classroom.

Should sets of informational texts be difficult to obtain, a good alternative is using printouts from Readinga-z.com, which has hundreds of downloadable informational texts at all ability levels. The cost is about a hundred dollars for the year, which hopefully can be covered by your school. Each "book" can be printed either single- or double-sided to create a small paper book when folded according to directions. These books include many of the same text features as the guided reading sets, such as a table of contents, bolded key vocabulary, photographs and diagrams, and glossaries. If printing in color is not feasible, you could consider giving students time, after teaching one of the introductory HART lessons described in this chapter, to color in the covers, with each student taking responsibility for particular sets of books.

Readinga-z.com also has a large collection of titles that are translated into Spanish. Although there are many ways HART can be differentiated for English learners in your classroom, one option for Spanish speakers in particular, depending on their level of proficiency, is to provide them with titles in both Spanish and English. By first reading the text in Spanish, students can more fully connect with the content, which gives them a rich foundation to comprehend both the concepts and specific vocabulary in the English version. There is also extensive research that supports the idea that developing literacy skills in students' native language positively supports literacy development in English (Cummins, 1979; Goodrich et al., 2013).

In order for students to independently choose books from the HART library (or bins), it is important that there is some sort of leveling system. My personal preference, at least for students reading at a 3rd-grade level and above, is using colored dots to indicate a general grade level. In the HART libraries in the 4th- and 5th-grade classrooms at Tiger Academy where I work as a faculty-in-residence, for example, a yellow dot indicates 2nd-grade level, a green dot is 3rd-grade level, a blue, 4th-grade, and red is 5th-grade. Each student or HART team is assigned a color so they know which books they can pick. This color system is designed to create an environment of controlled choice so that students have some autonomy in choosing texts based on interest but within a range that they can comprehend. Teachers who already have a system for leveling their classroom library that is working well will likely want to continue with their same system.

When I introduce the colors, I do not make exact connections between color and actual grade level. Eventually students understand these colors have a progression and that groups are made according to these levels. I have found that what matters most is not the coding system per se but the general sense of respect that teachers set at the start of the year that in any given skill, whether that is reading or math or basketball or solving puzzles, we are all at different places, and we are all always learning.

Allowing students to choose their own books is one way to support autonomy, one of the key criteria for promoting intrinsic motivation (Reedy & Carvalho, 2021; Ryan & Deci, 2000). Some educators emphasize teaching students strategies for choosing books themselves. Helping students to independently assess books and ascertain whether or not it is an appropriate choice based on their ability to comprehend it is an important lifetime skill to nurture (Williams et al., 2008). That said, this is a skill that takes time to develop. And while interest is absolutely important when it comes to students choosing texts, it is essential that choice is also competence-enhancing; that is, it is a task that presents an optimal level of challenge (Evans & Boucher, 2015).

In my own classroom, it took me a while to realize that, no matter how many times I taught lessons on book choice or had posters reminding students about the five-finger rule (if you get to five words on a page you can't understand it's not the right level for you), I would constantly find students who were choosing books that were too hard for them, whether because they saw the movie, because their friend was reading it, they just liked the cover, or (as was often the case) they didn't want to be seen with what they considered a little kid's book. I have also seen the opposite dilemma: a 4th-grade student who reads on a 5th-grade level and is reading *Junie B. Jones* all week because she enjoys it. This case is less concerning as she is certainly comprehending the book, but she is not being challenged or stretched with this text, which matters as students move toward that big jump that happens in 6th grade with both independence and complexity.

Now is interest important? Of course it is! As is enjoying books. But if we expect high levels of attention and comprehension during independent reading, whether or not one is using HART, it is absolutely essential that students are reading books they can comprehend. If we want students to be doing lots of critical thinking, in their discussion and in their writing, then it is absolutely essential students are reading books they can comprehend. Structured choice honors the idea that choice matters for cultivating motivation but also honors the fact that having some boundaries not only makes choosing easier but allows students to make choices that support their comprehension and growth as readers.

Another decision to make about your HART library is how students will keep track of the books they choose. Will they get a copy of a book checklist (see Table 1.1) or use a section in their reader's notebook? Do you want them to return books to their bins or have a return box and a student librarian in charge of putting books back together with a rubber band before returning them to the bin? If hanging folders are used, then no rubber bands are needed as the expectation is that students simply return books to that folder at the end of each period.

READING SPOTS

Because students are in leveled groups, it's a good idea to assign groups of students to certain spots in the room. Spreading students out to different parts of the room not only gives them a welcome change after sitting at their same desks all day but, since talking is an important part of HART, not having groups right next to each other can alleviate distraction from other groups' conversations. The more comfortable and appealing the spots, which of course can also be used for other things like independent writing, the better. Beach chairs are a great option since they can be folded up and put out of the way when independent reading or writing is not taking place. I have also

Table 1.1. Sample HART Book checklist

Name _____

Teacher _____

HART BOOK CHECKLIST

Date	Title of Book	Plants & Animals	Weather & Nature	Space and Planets	Energy & Light	Government	History	World Cultures	Other

Figure 1.3. Students Reading in a HART Spot

bought large pillows for groups of students to bring to a corner of a room, the rug area, or even just outside in the hallway. Creating these types of spaces, however, goes beyond just providing a comfortable space. Giving children a chance to sit in chairs that we ourselves would sit in at home or at the beach reflects the authenticity of this literacy task: it "replicate(s) or reflect(s) reading and writing activities that occur in the lives of people outside of a learning-to-read-and-write context and purpose" (Duke et al., 2006, p. 346).

The reality is that not every group of students can have an ideal HART spot, but at the very least they can move to a different area other than their desk. One group, for example, can meet at a guided-reading table, while another group pulls their chairs together in a circle. You can also have a rotating schedule so that students change their assigned HART spot once a week or once a month. I find it helpful to give each HART spot a name such as the Office (the guided reading table), the Beach (the beach chairs), or the Conference Room (the circle of chairs). This naming solidifies an area and does save time rather than describing an area, which is particularly helpful if you create a chart to keep track of rotating spots. But I also find giving each place a name makes it more fun for students. They love saying they are going to the "Conference Room," a sentiment that would probably not be true for just a circle of chairs.

TEACHING TRANSITIONS TO HART SPOTS

Once you have decided on groups of students and have leveled and organized your books, you are ready to start teaching students the expectations of HART. Detailed lesson plans for all HART lessons described in this book can be found in Appendix A. Any building of anticipation before you start teaching this new reading format is, of course, a plus. One way to do this is to keep the new part of the classroom library, or wherever you will be keeping HART bins, off limits until you teach your first lesson. You could even drape a sheet over this section with a sign that says, "HART Books: Grand Opening Next Week."

The first lesson for teaching HART focuses on introducing this new reading format to your students and teaching expectations for moving from desks to HART spots. If you have put up a sign saying "HART Library Coming Soon!" you can keep them guessing about what HART stands for, which hopefully piques their interest. But on this first day you want to be explicit about what each letter in HART stands for and why you are doing it. You might share some of the reasons described in the previous chapter about differences between reading stories and informational texts as well as differences between reading expectations in their grade and where they will be in a few years, whether your students are in 4th grade or 8th grade.

In this first lesson students also get an overview of the four main parts of HART: What Do You Know?, the Word Quiz, Read and Share, and reader's notebooks. With the steps visible to all students, either on a screen or an anchor chart (see Table 0.1 in the Introduction), briefly describe what each one is. You want to emphasize the reason they will be spending time practicing each step one at a time is because they are eventually going to be in charge of running each step on their own. This first day is also a good time to teach students to practice vocabulary related to being independent, such as facilitate, self-facilitate, and autonomous: where have they heard these words before? What do they mean? Then connect their understanding of these terms to how HART differs from a whole-class conversation.

The rest of this first day should be spent on teaching students about HART teams and how book choice will work. Like any type of reading that goes beyond pulling out a book and silently reading, it is much better if management expectations are not just explained but also explicitly modeled and practiced. After students learn what groups they are in and their assigned color or level, you can move on to teaching and modeling expectations for transitioning to HART spots with a description of the signal for moving, how long it should take, what to bring, the names and places of the different reading spots, and which group is going where.

After any minilesson, it's helpful to include a quick turn and talk afterwards so students can cognitively process the lesson in some way before there is any actual physical practice. This quick exchange of ideas allows all students to talk about and process the point of the lesson, but having this as a consistent expectation also affects accountability and attention during the lesson (Hale, 2008). It's just human nature that when an 8-year-old or a 15-year-old knows that, in a few minutes, she will have to verbalize what the lesson is about, she is more apt to listen attentively during instruction.

In this lesson about transitions, for example, I might say, "Turn to the person next to you and tell them what the expectations are for getting into your HART groups," or "Tell the person next to you where you are going when it's time for HART." Then after 20 seconds or so I ask one or two students to briefly share with the class what they and their partner said, confirming their answer or offering some adjustment. Since this lesson is about movement, I might also give a second, more physical prompt in which I say, "Great. Before we practice getting into spots, I want to see if you know exactly where you are going. We just went over which HART spot you are going to. So, on the count of 3, everyone point to where you are going to go. Ready? 1, 2 ,3 . . ." And what results (ideally) is a beautiful crisscross of arms reflecting every student's understanding of where they will go. After this, they are ready to actually practice their transitions.

MINILESSON: CHOOSING BOOKS

The next lesson, whether it follows the management lesson above or whether I teach it the next day, is about how students choose their books. If needed, you can first describe the way the library is organized and how the leveling system works, especially if it is new for this class. You can also pass out a book checklist (Table 1.1) to explain how the books are organized and how each bin category corresponds with the categories on the form. Give students a minute to read over the categories and then ask what they notice about how they are grouped. Explain how the book list will give them a bird's eye view of what categories they have not yet read.

Students should understand that, although all groups will be choosing a book at the same time on this day, eventually each group will be on their own timeline of when to choose a new book. Explain that once a group decides what topic they might like to read about, one person from the group looks for a set of books that matches their assigned color. In the guided practice phase of this lesson, each group has a team member come up to the library to choose a set. When students return to their group, everyone should check off the appropriate category and write in the title of their new book. Another option is for students to write down their book choices in a designated section of their reader's notebook.

Because this lesson on teaching book selection expectations is rather brief, and since students are already in their HART spots, it's easy to move on to the next lesson, which teaches students the first official step of HART called "What Do You Know?" The next chapter describes how to teach this step, in which students learn how to facilitate talk about background knowledge, and discusses why HART creates a highly supportive context for scaffolding ownership of this and other literacy skills.

CHAPTER 2

Scaffolding Prior Knowledge

When my twins, Emma and Leo, turned five last year, their older cousin Jake gave them a T-ball set. Emma was disappointed. Before teaming up with her brother to rip off the balloon wrapping paper, she squealed and made clear her hope was that it might be a Barbie princess castle. Once the T-ball set was revealed, her hopes were dashed. Leo, on the other hand, loved it. He didn't quite understand what T-ball was, but the picture of the boy with the large yellow bat hitting a ball was enough for him.

We had tried playing baseball earlier that spring with the plastic bat we already had. The twins first watched as their father, Xavier, had their older brother, Dexter, stand with the bat and explained how to hold the bat, where to put your feet, and how to stand. Then they watched as Dexter first missed and then hit a few soft throws from his dad.

"Okay I get it!" Leo shouted as he ran over and reached for the bat. "Can I try now?" I looked over at Emma who was squatting down, suddenly engrossed in picking blades of grass. The next 20 minutes were spent with Leo attempting to hit the balls Xavier threw him, which he did once, and encouraging Emma to give it a try too. After a few swings of just air, her previous lack of interest turned to total disinterest and pleads to go do something else.

I am not sure why I didn't think to get them a T-ball set myself. But once Jake took the twins out to the back yard, it was a completely different scenario. After Jake reminded Leo how to stand and hold the bat, Leo was able to hit the ball with the first swing and it went far. After a laugh full of pleasure and a "Yeah boy!" he was ready for the next hit. When it was Emma's turn, she also hit the ball, which was followed by a shy smile. Then she picked up the bat and got ready again. Like many types of classroom instruction, my experience of initially teaching our twins baseball involved different types of support that ranged from modeling and direct instruction to independent practice. The addition of the T-ball set reflects the critical middle step of scaffolding, the bridge that allows, or at least more easily encourages, transfer from teaching to independent practice.

In reading instruction, the concept of scaffolding is not new. The term, first attributed to Wood et al. (1976) in a teaching context, has become commonplace in schools, curricula, and professional development. The scaffolding metaphor to describe academic temporary assistance has a visual appeal as "it connotes a custom-made support for the 'construction' of new skills, a support that can be easily disassembled when no longer needed" (Stone, 1998, p. 344). This concept of learning is also reflective of the social, interactional theories of learning presented by Vygotsky (1978) and Pearson and Gallagher's (1983) gradual release of responsibility.

From prekindergarten to high school, there are numerous ways to scaffold student reading with varying interpretations of how to do it effectively. Researchers also emphasize a difference between planned scaffolding in reading, such as Guided Reading instruction, and contingent scaffolding, which reflects the more in-the-moment support given by teachers in response to observations of student comprehension, such as during read aloud conversations (Hammond & Gibbons, 2005). As discussed in the introduction of this book, despite the prevalence of different types of scaffolding in classrooms, this practice often reflects the middle of the gradual release of responsibility continuum (see Figure 0.1) where students practice a strategy with direct coaching from the teacher. There is no question that this is a critical and necessary step in supporting students toward independence. But what is often missing in classrooms is that next step when students practice a skill *on their own.*

So why does this matter? Because at this stage, between guided practice and independence, students have to take on more ownership for initiating a task, which has repercussions for not just developing skills, but for creating a learning experience that fosters feelings of competence and autonomy, two key ingredients for supporting intrinsic motivation (Ryan & Deci, 2000). In the case of Emma and Leo, there was something about being the ones in charge of hitting the ball and deciding when to swing yet being set up in a way that made hitting the baseball achievable that made them both not just enjoy the sport, but feel competent. That feeling of competence is key because it is what drives someone to want to keep doing a task.

ACTIVATING BACKGROUND KNOWLEDGE

The next step in HART, What Do You Know?, embodies this concept of giving students more ownership in practicing a familiar and widely taught reading strategy. Before an informational read aloud, for example, most teachers understand the importance of activating students' prior knowledge about a topic, often through a class conversation or even a written activity such as a KWL chart where students list and discuss what they Know, what they Wonder and what they Learned about a topic (Ogle, 1986). A similar prior knowledge activation occurs at the start of guided reading through conversation about the book while doing a picture walk or looking at the cover.

This step of activating background knowledge rests on the idea of schema theory, which states that when encountering new information, each reader goes through an iterative process of retrieving information and combining this new information with what he or she already knows (Rumelhart, 1980). This act happens naturally during reading. After all, it is not the text itself that contains meaning, but rather our individual mental representation of that text that leads to comprehension and construction of meaning (Kintsch, 1988). But there is substantial evidence that explicitly activating prior knowledge about a topic *before* one encounters text can substantially strengthen connections between prior and new information. This step is arguably even more important for English learners as drawing on prior knowledge may help overcome any deficits in academic vocabulary recognition (Hwang & Duke, 2020).

Despite the frequency with which teachers have students think about what they already know in read-alouds or guided reading, it is questionable how often students do this same task with any thoroughness when reading independently. In HART students are taking part in this same activity but, because it is self-initiated, it takes place further down the gradual release continuum. This self-initiation is critical. Although any stimulation of background knowledge before read-alouds or guided reading is beneficial, the act of thinking about prior knowledge is reflexive, not productive. Meaning, when a teacher asks her class, "So what do you already know about bears?" *she* is the one stimulating her students' memories of information and images of bears. This type of scaffolding is undeniably important. But in order for transfer to occur, it matters greatly that there are other times when *students* are the one asking those "what do you already know?" questions themselves. Unlike some prior knowledge tasks that might be geared more toward a collective building of a topic, such as before a whole-class read-aloud, the HART task has a dual focus of both activating prior knowledge about a particular topic before reading *and* developing student ownership and autonomy with that skill.

TEACHING "WHAT DO YOU KNOW?"

Once students have learned how to choose and document their book choice, the next step is to model and teach the What Do You Know? step. I like to be explicit about the fact that looking at the cover and talking about what you already know is probably something they have done many times before. You can also check their understanding of the purpose of this task by asking them to turn and talk to a partner about why we do this. What is the point of talking about what you know about a subject before reading?

After debriefing the "why" of talking about what you already know before reading, which likely will touch on stimulating background knowledge,

making connections, thinking about what you wonder, and better comprehending text, the next step is to highlight to students that, even though this
is something they have done before, they will be the ones to initiate it in
HART. You can use the "now that you are older, you get to be in charge"
angle to put a positive spin on this new expectation of autonomy.

Then, directing their attention to the cover of a book, whether on the
screen or in your hands, students can practice this step in their teams. You
might need to remind them that someone in the group has to initiate the
conversation by asking, "So what do you all know about bears?" It is also
important to remind students that they can share any information at all
related to bears (or whatever the topic of your model text is) even if it is
a past experience such as visiting a museum or seeing bear warnings on a
sign. Sometimes students feel they need to share specific scientific "facts,"
which can lead to very short conversations with some students not sharing
anything. But, if they understand they can offer any connection or association at all, it frees up their willingness to share and, in the process, sparks
their networks of knowledge.

After giving students a few minutes to talk, bring the class back together
and ask students to share what they talked about in their teams. What came
up in their conversations? At this point, it can be beneficial to point out that
we draw from lots of different spaces when thinking about our prior knowledge of a topic: personal experiences, other informational texts, history or
social studies classes, movies and television, and conversations at home or
with friends.

Now the practice moves from a shared text to the particular text that
each group has chosen. If students are already in their HART spots and
have chosen their texts, they are ready to go. If not, then give the signal for
the HART transition. As students talk, you can walk around and listen in
on groups, giving positive feedback or redirecting where necessary. Then
debrief as a whole class about how this step went. Because independence
is a main focus of this lesson, ask specifically about how the conversations
got going in addition to what they talked about—who initiated the conversation? How did the conversation go from there? At the end of the lesson,
draw students' attention back to where What Do You Know? is on the
poster, reminding them they just learned the first step in HART.

ENGLISH LEARNERS

Prior knowledge of a topic can greatly support comprehension of a text
for all readers but is especially important for English learners who are at
varying degrees of acquiring and recognizing English language vocabulary.
In one study researchers found that domain knowledge about a topic had a

much greater effect on reading comprehension of text for English learners compared to native English speakers (Hwang & Duke, 2020). Given that ELs are still developing familiarity with content vocabulary, not to mention other academic words and idioms in English, their background knowledge is more important in overcoming such deficits due to language learning. The wide reading of different topics they experience in HART can greatly support background knowledge development, which will, in turn, support subsequent comprehension of text, both narrative and informational. That said, you can also incorporate additional supports for ELs during this particular phase of HART so they can get the most out of each text they encounter.

One way to support ELs is to make sure you have some science and social studies texts in the HART library that relate to the cultures specific to the ELs in your classroom. For example, if some or most of your nonnative English speakers are from Mexico, try to get sets of books that reflect topics specific to that country. Some sets might include more general information about Mexico such as festivals and customs of Mexico and so would be put in a "Cultures of the World" bin. But there ideally are also books that would be found in other bins. For example, in a bin about history, you could include several copies of *The School the Aztec Eagles Built* by Dorinda Makanaoanalani Nicholson (2016), which describes a pilot squadron from Mexico that took part in World War II.

This inclusion of culturally relevant texts supports ELs in your classroom in two different but critically important ways. The first relates to the relationship described above between background knowledge and comprehension. Students who come from Mexico or whose parents are Mexican, for example, arguably have a much greater background knowledge of the topics they are about to encounter in the previously mentioned books compared to native English speakers, which gives them an advantage once independent reading begins. The other benefit has to do with the affective side of learning, which is both a complement to and a fuel agent for cognitive development. Including texts that reflect students' cultures and backgrounds is a validation and celebration of the experiences and knowledge they bring (Ebe, 2010). Not surprisingly, studies have found that including or increasing the number of culturally relevant texts in a classroom had a significantly positive impact on ELs reading engagement (Feger, 2006; Herrero, 2006; Stuart & Volk, 2002).

These findings point to the human nature of validation. When a teacher highlights characteristics of their students through choices she or he makes about what books are in the library, whether they reflect students' culture, their race, or sports they play, it creates a sense of not just belonging but of pride in the way one is unique. The key in the examples just listed, of course, is that some characteristics of children, such as race or culture, can be differences that are sometimes seen through a deficit model. Therefore, while finding ways to celebrate what makes each student unique and tap into their backgrounds is powerful with any child, it is particularly important to be aware of cultures and racial identities that are not traditionally represented. Using Bishop's (1990) metaphor of windows and mirrors, this awareness of cultural representation in the books in our library, although perhaps a more complex task with informational texts, benefits all our students.

Regardless of what countries your EL students originate from, it is valuable to find books that are not *just* about that country or culture. For example, if you have many Japanese students, it is wonderful to have books in your "Cultures of the World" bin about Japan, but there are ideally books in other bins that also have Japanese connections. Are there any books that describe scientific inventions or environmental initiatives in Japan? You can also consider biographies that feature men and women whose families originate from your students' countries. For example, if you have many Puerto Rican students in your classroom, whether they are ELs or not, you can include several biography sets about Supreme Court Justice Sonia Sotomayor, whose parents are from Puerto Rico, in your library.

We of course want all students, our EL students included, to go beyond topics they know well so they can develop the skills of connecting and thinking critically with a range of topics—those that are familiar and those are that are new. But having EL students start out with texts related to their personal background knowledge can be a way to build confidence as they are learning the steps in HART before transitioning to less familiar topics.

BUILDING BACKGROUND KNOWLEDGE

While What Do You Know? aims to stimulate background knowledge of a particular topic so students can get the most out of the particular book they are about to read, HART as a whole contributes to the development of students' background knowledge in general because it directly reflects the concept of wide reading, when students build knowledge by choosing and independently reading materials at their own reading level. Wide reading is one of the most productive ways to develop students' background knowledge (Fisher et al., 2016). Explicitly targeting this skill set starting in elementary schools is so important because accumulation of domain knowledge is inherently gradual and is not something that can be just be taught (Neuman et al., 2014).

This same concept of background knowledge as an ongoing, cumulative process is reflected in HART itself: What Do You Know? is an expectation not reserved for just when they choose a new book, but is how they will start off every HART time. If the book is not new, What Do You Know? is still very much about stimulating background knowledge before they open the book. But now, information they have already read becomes incorporated with their personal background knowledge. So each time what students know expands. For this reason, you can tell students that another option for starting off the What do you Know? conversation is asking each other, "What do you remember?" Creating time for students to do student-driven recall of information each time, even if for 2 or 3 minutes, not only strengthens background knowledge and a sense of accountability for comprehending what they read, but also creates a stronger foundation for the independent reading they are about to do (Hale, 2014).

CHAPTER 3

Scaffolding Attention to Vocabulary

When I worked as a literacy coach in the Boston Public Schools, all the literacy coaches in the district would meet for our own professional development every other Friday in the conference room of a Boston Holiday Inn. Most weeks we had an assigned reading meant to stimulate conversations about a specific topic in literacy. I remember one particular Friday, right after our usual ziti and salad lunch, when we were all given a small yellow and purple book about vocabulary instruction. "Oh great. Another book about teaching vocabulary," my friend Dyan said with clear sarcasm in her voice. "Hooray," echoed Connie, twirling her finger in the air but matching Dyan's lack of expression. Fast forward 2 weeks to our next meeting when we were all talking about this book, *Bringing Words to Life* by Isabel Beck, Margaret McKeown, and Linda Kucan (2013). And we didn't just talk about it during structured text discussions. We talked about the book as we stood in line to pour our morning coffee and during our ziti lunches. I even overheard conversations in the bathroom, from one stall to another—about vocabulary acquisition!

What prompted all this discussion was the fact that *Bringing Words to Life* created a new lens for many of us about language and how words are connected. For so long, my own understanding of vocabulary instruction had been relegated to lists of words that never seemed to be able to break free of the confines of memorizing and writing definitions and then using those words in a sentence. One of the most important takeaways from this book was understanding how important oral language use is for vocabulary acquisition. The idea of getting students to practice using words orally before asking them to incorporate them in writing makes so much sense: we are far more apt to use a word in writing if we have previously used it when speaking. Another learning outcome had to do with the importance of creating relevance for students by creating engaging and meaningful tasks with words and that doing so can help foster a curiosity about words. On the surface, this seems obvious. Of course we want to have engaging activities no matter what we teach. But previously my understanding of an engaging vocabulary activity was limited to creating a word search with vocabulary words or letting students make up a story with their words. Certainly there is nothing wrong with these activities, but looking back

I realize that I called them engaging when I was trying to create a "fun task" around vocabulary. Deep down I think I felt like vocabulary tasks were boring too. Not until I started implementing strategies from *Bringing Words to Life* did I realize vocabulary, *with the right conditions*, was engaging in its own right. The critical difference in these two types of engagement is that the latter one is far more apt to affect intrinsic motivation around vocabulary.

THE IMPACT OF GENRE

While vocabulary acquisition is a critical aspect of literacy development, regardless of what genre students are reading, it is particularly important, and more challenging, with informational texts. Not only do informational texts tend to have more unique and complex vocabulary words than stories of the same Lexile level, but they often do not follow a story arc—a structure that children are exposed to from the earliest years. So, with a fiction story, even when young readers are introduced to new characters, settings, or information, whether in a read aloud and when reading independently, this new information is propped up by a strong schema of story lines, plot development, and character interactions (Best et al., 2008). Due to the strong current created by story plot and characters, a reader may be able to keep comprehension intact even when they only have a partial understanding of unfamiliar words.

The lack of story structure in most informational texts means there is less of a comprehension foundation that can withstand a reader's difficulty recognizing unfamiliar vocabulary. Therefore, understanding content vocabulary plays a larger role in overall comprehension with informational text than with stories (Harmon et al., 2005). Although it is important that students learn and apply strategies for trying to make sense of unfamiliar words, too much time spent deciphering individual words increases the cognitive load of reading, rendering it less likely students will fully comprehend what they are reading (Kintsch, 1988; Santoro et al., 2016). What makes content vocabulary instruction particularly challenging is the wide variation of background knowledge that exists in each classroom, since every student brings with them a unique set of word knowledge based on their individual in- and out-of-school experiences (Blachowicz et al., 2006).

Most researchers agree that approaches to vocabulary acquisition need to be multi-faceted, that is comprised of both explicit and implicit supports for vocabulary learning. Students need direct instruction of new words but also authentic tasks in which they are exposed to, interact with, and use both familiar and new vocabulary. In terms of how these concepts are applied to classroom practice, Graves (2016) offers four key components of vocabulary instruction: (1) wide reading, (2) direct instruction of words, (3) word learning strategies, and (4) developing word consciousness.

The one component HART does not support is direct instruction of words. Nowhere in the following pages will you see descriptions for teaching or reviewing the meaning of words with students. The reason for this exclusion has nothing to do with its importance: Direct vocabulary instruction is widely understood as an essential facet of literacy instruction. This exclusion has everything to do with what HART is designed for, which is targeting the skills students use during independent reading. The design of this reading format is not meant to teach students new vocabulary but to create conditions in which students interact and attend to vocabulary *to their potential.*

What HART does do is complement direct instruction by supporting the other three tenets of vocabulary highlighted by Graves (2016). HART supports wide reading, since an inherent part of this format is that students are choosing books that represent a wide range of social studies and science topics. The Read and Share format, which will be discussed in more detail in the next chapter, supports word learning strategies since it is designed to heighten attention students give to words while they read, making it more likely they will use decoding and metacognitive strategies for figuring out unfamiliar words. This word learning is also supported by the fact that all students in HART are reading texts at their approximate reading levels; text complexity in relation to a student's reading ability is one of the key conditions that will either support or hinder students' ability to derive word meanings (Anderson & Nagy, 1993).

The last concept, developing word consciousness, or word curiosity, which describes the characteristic of being curious and interested in words and their meaning (Graves & Watts-Taffe, 2008), highlights the importance of addressing the affective side when it comes to vocabulary teaching and learning. In HART, developing word consciousness is most explicitly supported by the next stage of HART called the Word Quiz, when students preview upcoming content vocabulary words and discuss what they know about select words. This stage is less about an actual assessment and more about getting students to think about the vocabulary in their book. Even though it is not a quiz in the conventional sense, calling it a quiz solidifies it as an expected step and makes it more of an official task. But because the Word Quiz is done in a small, social setting, and because students have autonomy in choosing the words to talk about, there is an element of fun that is not always present in traditional vocabulary tasks. This relaxed, social setting, coupled by accountability because of the size of the group, matters not just for students freely talking about words but also for creating curiosity.

Table 3.1 describes the three types of word quizzes students can do with their teammates: Glossary Quiz, Word List Quiz, and Word Search.

Table 3.1. Word Quiz Options by Type of Text

Type of Quiz	For Texts That Have	Description
Glossary Quiz	A glossary	One student chooses 3–5 words from the glossary to ask the group. After a group-initiated discussion about each word, the student reads the glossary definition out loud. Students can also take turns choosing a word to discuss.
Word List Quiz	A list of featured vocabulary but no glossary	One student chooses 3–5 words from the list of content vocabulary to ask the group. Students can also take turns choosing a word to discuss. In a group-initiated discussion, students talk about what they know about each word.
Word Search	No glossary or word list dedicated to content-specific vocabulary	Each member of the group chooses 1–2 words (bolded words, if the text has them) in the text to discuss with the group.

Lessons in Appendix A describe how this step, along with What Do You Know? can be taught. See Appendix C for a Word Quiz handout that can be provided to students to remind them of the different Word Quiz options. The decision of which quiz to do will be driven by the type of text a team has chosen. Regardless of what type of quiz students do, students should understand that they, not the teacher, are in charge of choosing the words to talk about and starting the conversation about those words. Students should also understand the emphasis is on stimulating prior knowledge about words, not about getting a word "right" or "wrong." As suggested in the lessons, you can teach students to use the phrase, "What do you know about the word . . .?" Compared to a more traditional quiz-related question such as "What is the definition of. . . ?" the first phrase implies that the goal is not to get the "correct" answer but to share any prior knowledge related to the word. Consistent with the ideas about word learning set out by Beck et al. (2013), this type of interaction with words starts with the student experience first and then builds meaning from there. Rather than reflect that vocabulary is about knowing the "right" answer, this type of question acknowledges that building vocabulary knowledge is inherently iterative, meaning we gradually build deep understanding. "Knowing a word" is not a binary concept of knowing or not knowing and our understanding of words comes in different layers, including recognition and understanding the context in which a word is used.

Glossary Quiz

This type of Word Quiz is for teams that have a book with an actual glossary in the back, a select list of content specific words that appear in the text, typically accompanied by a brief, student-friendly definition. One student in the team volunteers to be the "Word Quizzer" and chooses 3–5 words to ask the other students in their team or students can each take a turn being the Word Quizzer. The goal is to choose words that are central to the topic of the book but not so familiar that everyone knows the exact definition. After the designated Quizzer asks, "What do you know about the word . . .?", others discuss their under-standing of this word. Even in this scenario where there is an actual answer, stu-dents should know they can offer any type of information related to the word, whether it's a guess of a definition, a memory of a particular context in which they heard the word, or even just an acknowledgement that they have heard the word but are not sure what it means. After a minute or two of discussion, the Word Quizzer shares the definition as written in the glossary.

> *Child A (The Word Quizzer): Okay so what do you know about the word meteor?*
> *Child B: A meteor? Um, like, I think it has something to do with space. Or the solar system.*
> *Child A: Yeah, but it's a little more than that.*
> *Child C: Like a moon rock.*
> *Child B: Rocks from the moon?*
> *Child C: Is it something that moves in space?*
> *Child A: Okay the definition is 'A piece of rock that travels through space. When a meteor goes through the Earth's atmosphere, it burns at a bright light.'*
> *Child B: What?*
> *Child C: Oh! I get it. Okay you ever seen a shooting star? Okay it's like that.*
> *Child B: Oh. So they are the same thing?*
> *Child A: Yeah, I think so.*

Word List Quiz

This version of the Word Quiz is for teams whose book does not contain a glossary but does have a list of content-specific words in the front of the book. The main difference here, of course, is that there is no definition avail-able. The designated Quizzer still decides which words to pose to the group (or students take turns), using the same prompt, "What do you know about the word. . .?", and the team discusses any prior knowledge they have of that word. Since the Word Quizzer has no special access to a definition, the Quizzer joins in the conversation about each word.

Figure 3.1. Students Doing the Word Quiz

Word Search

The third version of the Word Quiz is for teams that chose a text that has neither of these vocabulary text features, a glossary nor a word list. In this version, there is no Quizzer in charge of deciding which words to discuss. Instead, each member of the team looks for one or two vocabulary words in the text that relate to the topic of the book, a task often made easier by the use of bold words in informational texts. Then each person on the team takes a turn asking the group about the word they chose, again beginning with the prompt, "What do you know about the word . . .?" The following transcript shows a Word Quiz using this version.

> *Child A: So what do you know about the Executive Branch?*
> *Child C: Not sure. Something with government.*
> *Child A: Have any of you heard that word before, executive?*
> *Child B: I don't think so.*
> *Child C: Yeah, like you know people who are in an office? The people in charge. They are called executives.*
> *Child B: So it's like people who work in offices?*
> *Child C: Yeah or maybe people who are in charge.*
> *Child A: So maybe both. Since people who are in charge usually have an office. Okay so Child B your turn to pick a word.*

Several times when I have explained this type of Word Quiz, a concerned teacher will ask, "Well, what if they get the definition wrong?" First, I acknowledge that this certainly can happen: students may make some guesses but never quite reach the full meaning of a word. But I also emphasize the importance of not comparing this activity to a whole-class or small-group vocabulary lesson, but rather to independent reading, because *that* is the reading context HART is trying to influence. The alternative, I point out, is not teacher support, but silent reading where students just start reading without thinking about any of the words they will encounter.

What HART supports is attending to words, whether before or during reading. What we want students to do when they come across an unfamiliar word is to give it some effort—to think about the meaning of word. And, I would argue, we want them to do this whether they figure out the definition or not. We want to encourage the *attempt*. During the Word Quiz, there is a good chance that, especially since there is a conversation, students will approach an accurate meaning. But if they don't, that is okay because the primary thing we are scaffolding at this time, in addition to exposure to and accumulating content-specific vocabulary, is the desired habits of mind of *attending* to and thinking about vocabulary. Additionally, discussion of words in which there is space to "not know" or not reach a correct definition, allows students to take risks in sharing what they know, which, in turn, leaves space for instilling that important quality of word curiosity.

As will be explained in more detail in Chapter 6, teachers can also give students feedback with either conferences or minilessons on using strategies to decipher meaning of unfamiliar words. For example, if a teacher listens in on a group who is discussing the word *photosynthesis* but not attempting to break this word into meaningful parts, he can remind students or explicitly model this skill, either right then and there with a conference or with a minilesson the next day, especially if he notices other groups could use the same reminder. Another additional support that can be used, especially for older students who are more adept at using a dictionary, is to allow the Quizzer to use a student dictionary for words no one in the group knows. But ideally there are clear guidelines as to when you do this, because simply skipping to this task would bypass the vocabulary muscle flexing we want students to do of reaching back into their mind and recalling what they know about a word.

Since there is no direct vocabulary instruction embedded in HART, it is important to be explicit about how and in what way this vocabulary activity supports vocabulary acquisition. As mentioned earlier, vocabulary acquisition is not simply a matter of exposing students to many words, but rather instilling both the knowledge of word-solving techniques and the desire to do so. Table 3.2 describes characteristics of the Word Quiz that foster both word curiosity and use of vocabulary strategies.

Table 3.2. Word Quiz Supports for Word Curiosity and Vocabulary
      Acquisition

Social Context	The small-group discussion in HART aligns with Vygotsky's socio-cultural theory (1978), which states that optimal learning occurs when social interaction is part of the meaning-making process. Because the Word Quiz takes place in a small-group setting, as opposed to a whole-class conversation, conversation about words takes on a social rather than instructional tone.
Low-Risk Environment	A key characteristic of the small-group format is that it creates a low-risk environment for offering ideas and asking questions, which is much more conducive to active thinking compared to whole-class instruction. For most students, especially English learners, the absence of scrutiny creates a freedom to think more freely and take chances about sharing ideas about words.
Student Autonomy	Autonomy is often seen as one of the key components to creating a teaching and learning environment supportive of student engagement and motivation (Ryan & Deci, 2000). One feasible way to bring choice into classrooms is to have structured autonomy, that is choice *within* structured guidelines (Jang et al., 2010). In the Word Quiz students are in charge of which words to discuss, but within a structure guided by the text features, bold words, word lists, or a glossary.
Opportunity for Talking	Also aligning with Vygotsky's socio-cultural learning model is the idea that language use is a powerful vehicle for cognitive development (Palinscar & Brown, 1984). The small-group characteristic of HART means that all students, not just those who eagerly raise their hands in class, benefit from the dialogic experience in which they get to use their expressive vocabulary, actively formulate ideas, and have their ideas heard.
Peer Feedback	In the Word Quiz, discussion about vocabulary is multi-directional, which allows students to build on one another's ideas and experiences with words. Through this more open discussion about words, students can clarify and make connections, an interaction that is not as easy to emulate in a whole-class conversation about vocabulary.
Equal Opportunity	One of the most important aspects of the Word Quiz is that *all* students benefit from the characteristics described above, not just those who are more motivated to participate in class conversations.

DIFFERENTIATING VOCABULARY SUPPORT FOR ENGLISH LEARNERS

For English learners, the use of oral language, both speaking and listening, is particularly important for promoting vocabulary growth. ELs often feel intimidated to speak or share ideas in class, which decreases the chance they will participate fully in whole-class discussion, even when encouraged (Guccione, 2012). An important characteristic of HART, in terms of encouraging language practice for all students, but especially ELs, is the low-risk environment that is created by the small groups but also by the task: when students whose first language is not English understand that there is no right or wrong answer in terms of sharing what they know about a word, they are more apt to actively think about and actually share what they know.

Since repeated interaction with vocabulary is particularly important for students learning English as a second language (McCauley & McCauley, 1992), teachers can have EL students interact with chosen vocabulary in ways that go beyond the structures of the Word Quiz. One suggested strategy is to have ELs keep a section in their reader's notebook where they write down the Word Quiz words so they can return to them after reading. If definitions are given, students can either write these down or they can just draw a visual next to each word to help them remember the meaning. The teacher can model how to use this list as a resource while reading, as well as how to revisit this list of words once they finish their book. They can use a protocol similar to the Word Quiz only now with the added question, "Do you remember how this word was used in the book?" By the time students reach this last step, they will have actively engaged with content-specific vocabulary four times and in a variety of ways: once when writing, once when reading, and twice when discussing the words.

Teachers of Spanish-speaking bilingual students, as well as those who speak Italian or French, can also support students in using their knowledge of cognates—words that are derived from the same root word and have similar appearances and meanings in two different languages. Spanish, similar to Italian and French and other Romance languages, is derived from Latin. Although English is a Germanic language, Romance languages have contributed greatly to the development of our language. Explicit instruction on cognate relationships while reading has been shown to be one way that Spanish-speaking students can enhance their own comprehension of text and accumulate vocabulary (August et al., 2005; Nagy et al., 1993).

In small groups, whether during HART or at other small-group instruction times, teachers can model and offer guided practice for using this "cognate awareness" as one reads. Essential with any teaching of cognate awareness is talking about false cognates, words that may look and sound the same in English and Spanish but have no meaning relationship, for example *rope* in English and *ropa*, which in Spanish means clothes. Students need to understand that skillfully using cognates requires one to use the context of the sentence to make a judgment about whether there actually is a shared meaning or not.

One important attribute of Spanish-English cognates is that they have been shown to be particularly useful with more scientific and complex vocabulary because there are many high-frequency words in Spanish whose English cognate is a low-frequency, more academic word (Graves, 2012). For example, a native English-speaking 2nd-grader who commonly uses the word *bug* may not recognize the more elevated term *insect* in their text, whereas the Spanish-speaking English learner might draw on the cognate *insecto*, which is a more commonly occurring word in their language. An interesting reason for this difference in complexity is because during medieval times, Latin was the language used by scholars and clergy, who were at the front of scientific developments and theories (Bravo et al., 2007). Even when scientists veered away from religion, the concept of elevating scientific terms in Latin, the derivational language of Spanish, remained.

Given that second language speakers are often seen through a deficit model when it comes to classroom instruction (Ruiz, 1984), teaching the strong relationship between academic and scientific language in English and Latin-derived languages such as Spanish, can be particularly powerful when it is taught to not just English learners but all students. Classroom environments benefit when native English-speaking children are made more aware of the strengths and "funds of knowledge" that English learners bring, especially in an academic context.

Another strategy to help Spanish (and Italian or French) English learners strengthen their cognate awareness is to teach them specific cognates of prefixes and suffixes (Graves et al., 2012). Even with older students, there is evidence that teaching morphological awareness, with both native English speakers and ELs, enhances students' ability to be more self-sufficient in word learning and reading comprehension (Crosson et al., 2019). Teachers can differentiate and strengthen this skill by focusing on language-specific cognates. For example, teaching EL students that the suffix "tion" or "sion" in English is the same as "cion" in Spanish can be helpful with numerous content-specific words like nation (nacion), generation (generacion) or operation (operacion).

FURTHER DIFFERENTIATION

Teachers may also want to differentiate Word Quiz expectations depending on the age of their students. Content teachers in middle and high school, for example, might use the Word Quiz format, in addition to the What Do You Know? stage, as prereading activities for grade-level texts students read in class. Teachers can offer guidance by listing the words they think are particularly important to comprehend a particular passage or content topic. After students talk in pairs, teachers can facilitate a brief whole-class discussion to check for understanding. In this way, teachers are supporting targeted content knowledge and students' access to upcoming text as well as ownership in thinking about words. Teachers in these grades can also have students write down these content-specific words and related definitions and then reinforce students' use of these terms through follow-up homework or in-class game-like activities.

Whether you are teaching elementary, middle, or high school students, the idea of discussing words before reading is not new. What makes the Word Quiz particularly powerful is who is in charge of this act. Similar to other aspects of HART, the Word Quiz stage resides in the not-always-occupied space of the Gradual Release of Responsibility (Pearson & Gallagher, 1983) where students apply practice on their own with opportunities for teacher feedback, increasing the likelihood they will transfer these skills when reading an informational text on their own.

CHAPTER 4

Scaffolding Attention While Reading

In Chapter 2 you read about Emma and Leo getting a T-ball set from their older cousin, Jake. One of the most powerful parts of that story may have seemed, at first, like just a detail. It wasn't when Leo got excited when opening the mystery box, or when either twin first hit the ball: it was when Emma, after hitting the ball, gave "a shy smile." So why is her smile so important? Because there is nothing more powerful in the learning process then how a person feels when he or she is doing that activity.

Emma and Leo's T-ball experience is at the heart of HART because both place a tremendous value on the role intrinsic motivation plays in getting better at something. Their story also reflects the differences that exist in schools. Like many students who come to our classrooms as motivated readers, Leo already had a certain level of motivation to learn how to play baseball. He already had both a positive perception of the sport and likely a positive self-perception that he would be good at it, which made him more excited to give it a try. These same characteristics are also what arguably made him more resilient when he missed a ball or encountered struggle. Emma, on the other hand, did not have that initial motivation to play this game. She did not already have an interest or particular motivation to learn to play baseball. And, while she did not necessarily have a strong negative self-perception of herself in terms of sports, she was certainly quick to say she wasn't "that good at baseball" compared to Leo. Her story is an important one since many students do not have a positive response when they hear it's time for reading or are given a book, a feeling that might even be stronger with informational texts. Perhaps they roll their eyes, feeling it is just a chore or, like Emma, see it as something they are "not really good at." Not only do these feelings change the initial motivation for doing an activity but, when struggle inevitably occurs (in either T-ball or reading), they are less likely than their motivated peers to persevere.

While the T-ball set helped Emma with the skill of playing baseball, what arguably was just as or even more important was that it simply *got her* to experience the reason why people love to play that sport. No amount of us telling her, "Emma, baseball is a great sport! You can play with your brothers! It will be fun!" could replace that sweet, satisfying feeling when you swing the bat and hit the ball with that great smack that propels it into the air. That feeling, that joy, is what made her smile. In a similar way, HART does not rely on explaining or telling students to read informational text with a high degree of attention or to monitor their thinking because it is important: it simply sets up a structure that *gets them* to this, which allows them to experience the joy of reading informational text to their potential. As Gambrell (1996) points out, in addition to teaching expectations around reading comprehension and metacognitive skills, we can also create structures that simply get students to experience what we are teaching.

The primary task in HART, the time when students alternate between reading and talking, is one of the biggest reasons why this format has the ability to affect engagement and motivation. The reason it "gets" students to experience engaged reading, however, is multi-layered. The next section first describes how HART as a whole supports student engagement by considering alignment with Ryan & Deci's (2000) self-determination theory, a widely applied theory of human motivation. The rest of the chapter focuses on the next and main part of HART when students read and talk: first with a description of what this independent reading component of HART looks like in practice and the different options for student-run conversations followed by a discussion of why student talk, particularly small-group talk, is such an important ingredient in high attention reading and the motivation-comprehension relationship.

COMPETENCE, AUTONOMY, AND RELATEDNESS

Similar to other reading formats that are designed to target engagement of reading, HART reflects the three criteria that are set forth in Ryan and Deci's (2000) self-determination theory (Figure 4.1): competence, autonomy, and relatedness. This theory posits that these three psychological needs are required to be present, whether in a school setting or not, in order for a person to feel intrinsically motivated. The utility of applying psychological theory to education is important because rather than simply stop at the idea that students need to be motivated to do well in school, which few would argue, it points to what needs to be present to affect change and why

Figure 4.1. Model of Ryan and Deci's Self-Determination Theory

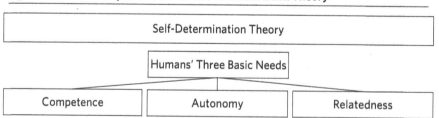

Table 4.1. Supports for Competence, Autonomy, and Relatedness in HART

Competence	• All students can access text. Students read books at or near their instructional reading level. • The task for talking (share one thing) is attainable for all students.
Autonomy	• Students have structured choice when choosing books. • Students decide what vocabulary to discuss. • Students decide what topic to read about. • Students initiate and facilitate discussions.
Relatedness	• Groups of students are small (3–5 students) and meet consistently. • Student-led discussions are social in nature. • Students talk and write about information that is most interesting to them.

attending to these less academic skills matters when planning teaching and learning tasks (Reeve, 2002).

What I love about this model is that it is grounded not in classroom instruction, but in the human condition. So often it seems conversations around education focus so much on standards and skills that the emphasis on engagement, motivation, and important concepts like academic self-perception get lost. Effective teachers certainly understand these are all important elements in teaching. But the narrative that exists at the district and state level matters: it creates a filter that can determine what district and school administrators focus on. What effective teachers also understand is that if we pay as much attention to student engagement and motivation as the content-related standards, we will have a far better chance of reaching those academic goals set out by the standards and, not unimportantly, have a better chance of creating curious, lifelong readers. Additionally, and this is the premise that HART is based on, once you can engage all levels of students in a meaningful way, you have buy-in. And there is no better ingredient than that to improve both the quality and quantity of reading students do.

Although there are many different ways teachers can support competence, autonomy, and relatedness, Table 4.1 shows how the overall design of HART aligns with these three criteria.

INDEPENDENT READING

The real key to high attention reading happens when students start alternating between independent reading and short segments of talk in which they discuss what they read. There are two main options of how to do this "Read and Share": students can move through the HART steps at the same time, or you can have students facilitate the movement between reading and talking on their own. In the first option, the teacher is the facilitator in terms of time—how long students do each task. The primary benefit in doing this is that all groups are talking and reading at the same time. Students still self-initiate conversations about what they read and they still have autonomy over what they talk about; they just don't decide when to move between reading and talking. The timing is facilitated by the teacher. The amount of time for each independent reading session will vary by grade level but it should generally start with smaller increments, maybe 2 or 3 minutes, and then be lengthened as students become better at reading with high attention. This concept of "starting small" reflects the fact that the primary focus is on the *quality* of reading and then, once quality reading becomes the habit, the *quantity*, the stamina, for reading can be lengthened, a concept that is discussed later in this chapter.

The second option, which might work for students who have already done HART, or for older students, is when each group moves through the HART steps at their own pace including What Do You Know? and the Word Quiz. For the Read and Share, rather than the teacher determining how many minutes of quiet reading everyone will do, each team, when they are done talking, decides where they will read up to next. There are different pros and cons for each choice, with autonomy rather than management of talking being the reason to have students run HART themselves. Some teachers may prefer to give teams their own timer to manage the transition from one component to the next. You can also give teams different amounts of minutes for the Read and Share portion to further differentiate HART.

For this second option it is particularly important to have groups spread out as much as possible and to teach lessons on how to run the Read and Share step on their own. An expectation that is likely new for students is that they, not the teacher, decide when to pause reading to talk. A good rule of thumb is to have students look for a stopping point a few pages ahead, perhaps to the end of a chapter or a particular heading, a concept that can be modeled and practiced in a lesson. Similar to the first option, this time frame is temporary and can be lengthened as students get used to this high attention reading. Lessons 5 and 6 in Appendix A reflect the first option for facilitating HART where students go through the steps at the same time. There are also two lessons in Appendix B for teachers who want their students to run HART at their own pace, in addition to an optional review lesson to further support independence.

The ideal scenario (if we are looking at HART from a purely autonomy-driven perspective) is that students move through each step on their own. But . . . that would be disregarding the other aspect of the human condition, especially with younger students, which is that there is simply more accountability to *not* talk when reading independently if everyone else is also

Figure 4.2. Students Reading Independently in HART

quietly reading. Even if a team is on task while reading, having other groups talking at the same time is just not the most conducive environment for the high-attention reading that we are trying to get students to do.

Regardless of which option you choose for HART, it is important to be explicit with students about the pace of their reading. Students should understand that being a faster reader is not the sign of a better reader: it's when you take your time reading that you are able to comprehend what you read to your potential. Sometimes reading assessments in the primary grades that test fluency with a timing component can have the unintended effect of students reading too fast or at least thinking that is the sign of a strong reader, even when they get to the upper elementary and middle grades. Certainly, there is some truth to that: when students are first learning to decode, a slow pace can reflect an overuse of decoding strategies to figure out words, which of course interferes with comprehension. But by the time students start reading around a 3rd-grade level, when both sentences and the information and ideas of sentences become more complex, the idea of keeping up with some sort of clock in terms of how fast you read the words becomes outdated. Far more important is a focus on teaching students that the new barometer should be on how well you understand, not how fast you can read.

Although emphasizing one's ability to comprehend over speed can help, students will of course still read independently at different paces, even when they are at similar reading levels. So students in the same group will not always stop at the same sentence, paragraph, or even page when it is time to share, especially if they are not choosing a particular place to stop as described in the second option. And that is okay. Even if there is some discrepancy in where they stop, it will likely be minimal. There will also still be a significant amount of shared understanding. Even in the case where one student talks about information that her groupmates have not yet encountered, the main elements of the share are still intact and the intended accountability is not diminished. To alleviate some of the possible "Hey, that's not fair! You're one page ahead!" comments, it can be helpful to call out this natural difference ahead of time, and even point out that a preview of upcoming information can only benefit comprehension.

One way to differentiate for students who read below grade level is to pair them up and have them alternate reading aloud. Although HART is designed to target the internal task of independent, silent reading, the reality is that in the upper elementary grades and even in middle and high school

Figure 4.3. Students Pair Reading During HART

grades, there are many students who still read far below their grade level. Informational texts below a 2nd-grade level are so dependent on picture support for any vocabulary and are read through so quickly that doing traditional HART with such low levels of text is either not as effective or can create management challenges.

In these instances, I would pull students aside and explain how to alternate their reading with one person reading aloud and the other one supporting them, not telling them words, but being like a teacher giving cues like "What makes sense there?" or "Look at the first part of the word." In this way, the two students reflect what occurs with a more mature reader, which is that one part of your brain is reading the text while the other part is monitoring. Additionally, reading this way creates an important accountability, especially for below–grade-level students, for attending to text while reading.

SHARE ONE THING

The type of talk that students do in between segments of independent reading, that is sharing "one thing" they learned or thought was interesting, is also deliberate. There is an important distinction between sharing one interesting concept and summarizing, another common talking task. Summarizing is generally understood as the ability to highlight or recall the main points or key information from a passage or text (Pressley et al., 1989). While this task can be helpful in getting students to synthesis a piece of text, it remains at a text-based processing state; that is, it does not require the reader to go beyond a recall or paraphrasing of what is literally stated in the text (Kintsch & van Djilk, 1978; Leopold & Leutner, 2012).

One of the greatest differences between summarizing and sharing what you learned is that there is an immediate personalization—a bridge that is unique between the text and the reader. Sharing one thing has a stronger relevance for students: what we decide to share depends on our own background knowledge, since what we personally find interesting is unique to each reader. "Sharing one thing" is also a more authentic task, something we as adults might do after reading an interesting article and talking about it with a friend. We might start out with a quick overall summary, but what we mostly do is share something that we found particularly interesting, which often leads to a conversation.

Another important characteristic of sharing one thing is that the task is doable, which is strongly connected to the authenticity of the task and to feelings of competence. There are many students who either would see summarizing what they read every time as a chore or not feel competent that they could do so or a combination of both. Since a primary purpose of HART is to get the wheels going on that self-perpetuating cycle of engagement and comprehension, the naturalness and "doableness" of the task matters.

The authenticity of the task also contributes to what often happens after students share things they learned or found interesting in HART, which is they start to share other types of thinking about this information. Sharing one thing, especially compared to summarizing, offers a much more natural segue into doing other types of thinking beyond literal. Consider the following excerpt of a group talking during the share portion of HART:

Child A: *So what did you guys learn?*
Child B: *I learned that at first people in the 1880s built a railroad to go across Panama to get things across.*
Child A: *Yeah, I didn't know that. That's crazy.*
Child C: *I know. I guess they used railroads a lot back then. But still, that would mean you would have to get stuff off a boat, on a train and then back on a boat?*
Child B: *So maybe that's why they decided to build a canal even though they finished the railroad.*
Child C: *Well if you look on page, hang on . . . 7 it says that they did it to make money.*
Child B: *Oh yeah. So, Child A what did you learn?*

This tendency to move from literal recall of information to thinking about that information is also a reflection of the genre. Learning about the world, whether it's how the heart pumps or how the Panama Canal works, is just really interesting! It's not unusual for students, after they share one thing, to react to each other's comments with shared reactions of surprise, which can spurn wondering questions and theories in answer to their questions. I have also noticed that students will, without any direction from me, naturally go back into the book to back up points or use diagrams to reiterate learning. The next chapter looks at how teachers can be even more intentional in encouraging this type of high-level and critical thinking in HART.

BUILDING STAMINA

While HART is designed to get students to experience reading informational texts to their potential, and in doing so, experience the joy of reading, it is still done in the service of traditional independent reading. Just like T-ball, HART creates a scaffolded version of "the real thing" that allows students to both develop the needed skills to do the task well while also creating enjoyment and a positive experience for that task. And just like T-ball, we don't have students do HART with the purpose that they stay there. The short time frame described above is meant to be temporary, to scaffold the internal muscles of reading to one's potential. In other words, once there is an explicit emphasis on quality of reading, you can start focusing on the quantity of reading, a little bit at a time, for whatever works for your grade and your students.

One important aspect of stamina for reading informational text, however, is that it is not a skill that gets developed in any one grade. I would caution against moving too quickly in extending the time frame, especially in the elementary grades where this high attention reading might be new. A 3rd-grade teacher, for example, may start off having his students read for 4 minutes at a time and might only move up to 6-minute increments after a month, with the intention of increasing the independent reading time each week after that. Meanwhile, a 7th-grade teacher might start with 5-minute increments of independent reading, increase that time to 7 minutes a few weeks later, and 10 minutes a few weeks after that. Teachers can also post a visual to reflect this goal of upping the amount of time students read in between talking such as a timeline with a paper arrow that moves.

Students should also understand that quality high attention reading is a prerequisite for moving the time. Since we cannot literally see whether this is happening in their minds, we have to rely on observable indicators of attentive reading, which goes beyond seeing that students are quiet and looking at their books. What are their eye movements? Are they tracking sentences with the return sweep that mimics the direction of the text? You can also get a sense of quality by the way students are talking during the share time. Are they able to recall information they just read? During independent reading you can also have some students quietly read out loud to you in a reading conference format. Not only is this a great teaching opportunity, but it can also help to give a sense of how they are reading independently. As will be discussed in Chapter 6, the Read and Share format alone will not necessarily produce high attention reading: it needs to be coupled with reinforcing this expectation with consistent monitoring and feedback.

The amount of time that students talk can also fluctuate. My suggestion is to, at first, keep the time for talking the same since the real focus is on increasing students' stamina for independent reading. But, as will be discussed in the next chapter, the more you increase expectations for the type of talking and thinking students do in between segments of reading, the more time you might want to give students to talk. Eventually, HART might resemble the visual in Table 4.2 where most of the Read and Share time is taken up with reading with a midway break (an "intermission") and a final share before they move on to reader's notebooks. I would caution teachers in the elementary grades in particular to not move too quickly toward this goal or feel that you need to reach this at all. Although independently reading informational text for extended periods of time is the eventual goal, as stated before, this is a skill that takes time to develop.

Some teachers might also decide that after several months of HART, especially if it's a daily activity, they want to transition back to traditional independent reading where students choose their own books, either fiction or

Table 4.2. HART Schedule With Intermission

What Do You Know?
Word Quiz
Independent Reading
Intermission Share
Independent Reading
Final Share
Reader's Notebooks
Share

nonfiction. You can still have students talk to each other about their books during an intermission. I find that even with traditional independent reading the inclusion of an intermission not only acknowledges the physical need for a break, but also helps sustain attention over time. This type of conversation will not have quite the same benefits without a shared experience of reading the same text but, at this point, you would be making a deliberate focus on independence.

WHY SO MUCH TALKING?

So far in this book, I have described many different ways to include student talk in processing different literacy skills: background knowledge, vocabulary, literal comprehension and—as will be described in the next two chapters—critical thinking. HART is grounded in Vygotsky's (1978) sociocultural theory, which suggests optimal learning takes place when language use is social and interactive. But I also acknowledge that, for some teachers, making a transition from more teacher-directed lessons or from traditional independent reading where the classroom is quiet is not always easy. The sound of different groups of students talking about different topics may sound . . . messy. When students talk in HART about what they know or about what they read, the room is definitely not quiet.

For teachers who are not used to it, seeing student-run talk this way does requires a shift in what is valued. After all, there is something counterintuitive to the idea that noise is more desirable than a controlled class conversation where everyone can hear what is said, and the teacher is there to correct any "wrong" answers. And I do sometimes need to have reminders or group conferences (with certain teams of students) on how to have conversations without getting so loud you are distracting other groups. But once you start listening to the "noise" of this talk, it becomes something quite wonderful. Because you hear *every* student actively processing ideas.

It's also about what you see. Often accompanying the talk are those smiles I mentioned earlier that are not just a nice side effect but a critical part of hooking students into whatever task they are doing. And what we believe matters. Not only are students capable of having productive, academic conversations, but students are more apt to live up to those expectations when they sense our trust that they can have worthwhile discussions without constant guidance (Michaels & O'Connor, 2012).

In any workshop I give that involves student talk, to emphasize the value of this trade-off, I always share a slide of four different brain scans that show brain activity when a person is seeing words, listening to words, speaking words (i.e., repeating words), and producing words. The amount of activity in the scan that shows production of language is visibly and remarkably larger and more colorful than any of the other slides. This pronounced activity is due to the fact that talking about one's ideas, as opposed to just listening or thinking, or even repeating what is said, is cognitively more demanding: the act of producing language requires numerous processes from several different parts of the brain. Unlike active listening, speaking requires both language comprehension and language production, which results in deeper processing of information (Cazden, 2001). In addition, actively contributing to discussions stimulates students' background knowledge and expressive vocabulary (Michaels et al., 2008; Vasilyeva & Waterfall, 2011). When seeing these brain images, it is hard to refute how much more "alive" the brain is when a person, whether a child or adult, is forming and saying words based on their own thoughts.

WHY TALK IN SMALL GROUPS?

While creating more opportunities for student talk is always a positive, it is also important to consider the different contexts of talk. Similar to literature circles, HART is done in small groups that are not only social in nature but, because of their size, encourage interaction by all members. Compared to whole-class conversations that tend to reflect the teacher-directed Initiate-Response-Evaluate (IRE) discourse, these smaller spaces create a powerful environment where *all* students in that group have a chance to verbalize their ideas. This concept of everyone actively talking instead of passively listening is incredibly important. Both children and adults, of course, learn many things by listening to others. But it takes intention and effort on the part of the listener to take the words we hear other people speak and absorb those ideas. While we can certainly discuss listening expectations with our students and create conditions that encourage them to actively listen to one another during whole-class discussions, relying *only* on this type of talk disregards the human nature of listening (there is only so long one can do it actively) and the different motivation levels in our classrooms. And, as the previously mentioned brain scans show, even the best listening can never match the active thinking that occurs when talking.

Creating small spaces for talk is also a matter of equity. Students who tend to do the talking in whole-class conversations, especially in the IRE type of discourse, tend to be the students who are more motivated, speak English as a first language, and have positive self-academic concepts. Thus begins the often occurring, although often not intended, vicious cycle of the Matthew effect, in which the "rich get richer and the poor get poorer" (Stanovich, 1986). In this case, those who would arguably benefit the most from talking and all it brings—engagement, expressive vocabulary, and active processing of ideas—are the ones least likely to raise their hands to speak, which further widens academic and affective trajectories.

Students of any age, especially second language learners and students with low academic self-concept, also benefit from small-group or pair talk because it reduces anxiety and self-consciousness that can inhibit active thinking. This reduction in anxiety is critical because it literally frees up students' minds. Our brains are wired to protect us from threat in any form, even when it is emotional or psychological. Any energy that could be spent on higher-order thinking gets rerouted to deal with this emotional threat. Have I seen teachers facilitate literature conversations that are engaging and attempt to involve everyone? Absolutely—and it is a pleasure to watch. But there is a difference between engaging teaching and student engagement. The fact is no matter how caring, engaging, and wonderful a teacher is, it is simply a matter of human nature that, as the audience of talk becomes bigger, the differences in how students feel about speaking their ideas start to emerge.

One of the best features of small-group talk is that, in addition to creating a space that encourages participation from more reluctant students, it also creates a heightened sense of accountability for all levels of students, which in turn affects attention and active processing. Important to point out is that this accountability is not teacher-driven, but peer-driven. This is an important difference because it supports one of those key conditions for intrinsic motivation: autonomy (Ryan & Deci, 2000). Even if groups were small, students would arguably not be as engaged if the teacher gave each group a list of questions they had to ask each other about their books. According to Ushioda (2011), who studies the connection between motivation and autonomy, autonomy matters "because it is a way of encouraging students to experience that sense of personal agency and self-determination that is vital to developing their motivation from within" (p. 224).

Strategically promoting autonomy in classrooms often leads to one of the other conditions for intrinsic motivation, competence, which Ryan and Deci (2000) define as the feeling of mastery of a task. In some ways, autonomy can be seen as a prerequisite for competence since in order to feel a sense of efficacy or capability, there has to be an understanding that it is you who did the task and not someone else. Emma or Leo, for example, would not feel a sense of competence if each time they hit the ball, I stood behind them, held their hands in mine, and swung the ball with them. Doing this with them may provide valuable scaffolding, but it is not until I let go, and they try it on their own, that either of them would start to feel a sense of competence.

The same is true in classrooms. We need direct instruction and scaffolding through things like small-group instruction. But when we also allow space for students to try things on their own, and accept that they will make mistakes when doing so, we not only see what they are truly capable of, but we set the stage for that sense of competence. In HART, and other types of student-led formats, such as literature circles, students are truly in charge of the discussion. What often surprises many teachers when they listen in on these small-group conversations is what smart things students say without teachers' immediate input or help.

WHY READ AND SHARE?

The above section answers the question, why does talking in small groups matter? But why alternate talking and reading? How does that help with comprehension? Shouldn't students read for as long as they can? The first part of the answer to these questions has to do with the brain's capacity for taking in new information. For many of the nonfiction texts that children read, most, if not all of the information, is new. And as has been discussed previously, reading information compared to stories simply takes a lot more internal effort. Just by pausing the flow of incoming information, the brain has time to digest and solidify that information before moving on to more new information (Harvey & Goudvis, 2007). Including consistent breaks from taking in new information allows students time to process and synthesize information they read and also creates a fair expectation of high-quality reading.

The real power of alternating talking and reading with informational texts, however, lies in how the imminent expectation of having to talk about what you read affects how students attend to the text. While the production of language is important in its own right, it is the *expectation* of talking that most impacts the way students read independently. A similar phenomenon exists with speaking. In one interesting study (Carota et al., 2009) neuroscientists took brain images during both active talking and periods where there was intention to talk, that is, a person planned to talk but never actually said any words. What they found was that even during the intention to talk, there was more activity occurring in the brain than during periods of listening. This makes sense. Think about this scenario. You are at a friend's house for a birthday party, standing in the living room with two other people talking about a recent current event. As you listen to one person talk, you think of a really good counterpoint. Suddenly someone announces it's time for the birthday cake and to hurry up and come into the kitchen. Your conversation comes to an abrupt stop, and you all head to the other room. While you never actually said the words to describe what you were thinking, your brain, *thinking* it was going to talk, was actively working to form the language to express those ideas.

The party scenario would be a very different experience had you been at the same party, listening to someone stand up and give a speech. You might be actively thinking about your own thoughts in relation to what this person was saying (our minds are always active, after all), but without an expectation that you would be contributing to the conversation at some point, it just would not be at the same level. The small size of the group in the first scenario dictated an implicit, social expectation that you would be contributing to the conversation. Likewise, in my own college classes I remember I often thought about what I might say in response to what a professor or a peer said, but unless I raised my hand, an action that created an expectation that I would talk, my mind didn't go past a certain level of concretely formulating ideas. HART is designed to create a talking environment that is big enough to create a social environment where different perspectives and thinking can be shared but small enough to preserve this sense of accountability and heightened attention *while reading independently* due to the upcoming expectation of sharing what is learned.

This concept of heightened attention due to expectations, and not teacher expectations but one powered by human nature, creates a wonderful snowball relationship between cognition and engagement. In such a setting, students are more likely to attend to text and use the metacognitive skills and do the types thinking we hope for and teach, while at the same time how much students are actively processing ideas about a text has direct repercussions for student engagement and motivation (Guthrie & Taboada Barber, 2011).

Another important characteristic of this part of HART is that the task of reading, initially, is short. This may seem counterintuitive as one of the overall goals of this reading format is to increase stamina with independent reading. But as described above, the goal is to focus *first* on the quality and *then* build the quantity. When students start reading in HART, there has to be, at least initially, a sense of imminency in order to feel that expectation of talk. When a 9-year-old knows that in about 3 or 4 minutes she is going to be talking to a peer about what she just read, it is natural that she reads with heightened attention. So it is the peer talk, *coupled* with texts that all students can comprehend *and* a doable, upcoming task, that is the driving force of HART.

And this is where the magic happens. Because it is in the act of reading at a high level that students are most likely to experience the intrinsic reward of reading, a lot like Emma felt when she hit the ball. She had to feel what the joy of baseball was like for herself in order to buy in to doing the task. So it's creating and, in a sense, manipulating an *experience* in which students experience both the capability of and pleasure in reading that no amount of a teacher telling students why reading is important or reading is enjoyable will ever come close to doing.

CHAPTER 5

Scaffolding Critical Thinking

Has it ever taken you longer to put two and two together to make four than it should have? For me, that happened with the connection between the way students were reading informational texts and the way they were writing about them. Remember Dante, the 5th-grader who loved his book about sharks but was not really *reading* the text? He was also one of the students who was not a big fan of writing in his reader's notebooks. He would often use one of the more common procrastination tactics: getting up to sharpen his pencil many times, asking to go to bathroom, or looking in his desk (for what I am not sure). And when he did write, he would write only a few sentences before copying sentences from his book. He did not really see anything wrong with this. As he explained when I asked him why he didn't just put the same information in his own words, "Because I am supposed to write what the book is about!"

Dante, of course, was not the only student over-relying on his book during reader's notebook time. After the 5th-grade teacher and I both realized this trend, we responded with several reader's notebook lessons on the importance of putting facts in your own language and talked about how to use your book as a supportive resource without copying exact sentences. We even talked about plagiarism and why it's important not to use the exact words someone else wrote. Weeks after I had my ah-ha moment about Dante's "sort of" reading, it suddenly dawned on me: of course he is over-relying on the book! If he is only doing that "sort of" reading, then how can he rely on what's in his head? The same is true for expectations in relation to writing about your thinking: how can we expect students to think critically about what they read through writing if there isn't a basic literal understanding of what is in the book in the first place?

Suddenly it seemed so clear. Spending all that time and energy on writ-ing about reading or thinking critically about what you read was going to be like putting water in sieve, at least for those who were doing that "sort of" reading. It was, once again, another example of the Matthew effect (Stanovich, 1986) at play—those who were already motivated or used to reading informational text as fluently as stories would be better able to syn-thesize, connect to, and remember what they read, which would translate into higher-quality reader's notebook writing.

There had been so much emphasis (perhaps deservedly so) on teaching comprehension skills and critical thinking, that the very simple concept of also attending to students' literal comprehension seemed to have gotten lost. Not surprisingly, this delayed realization only fueled my determination to find a way to tap into that completely independent and seemingly untouchable space in students' heads when it is just them and the books in their hands. That said, this is not a "throw the baby out with the bathwater" suggestion. We want to always be thinking about how we can bring critical and higher-order thinking into the tasks our students do, anywhere in the curriculum. But literal comprehension provides an incredibly important platform for the thinking that we want students to do. And while research points to a continued overuse of recall and literal questions in reading instruction, the need to bring more critical thinking into teaching and learning will be stronger if we attend to all levels of the comprehension spectrum (Hale & Kim, 2020).

The fact that HART does not have an explicit focus on high-level thinking does not by any means indicate it does not or cannot support this type of thinking. In fact, it does so in three distinct but complementary ways: during independent reading, during the talking, and when students write in their reader's notebooks. This chapter first describes how HART supports inferential thinking through the Read and Share format and then how the addition of reader's notebooks can extend and deepen critical thinking about informational texts even further.

DURING READING

The first way HART supports inferential thinking has to do with the format's explicit focus on motivation and attention to literal comprehension. It may sound counterintuitive that one way that HART supports deeper thinking is by *not* focusing on it, but as mentioned previously, this has to do with the inherent relationship between motivation to read and the thinking we do while reading. Thinking while you read is something that naturally occurs with motivated readers. There is ample research to back up the strong relationship between motivation and reading comprehension proficiency (Guthrie et al., 1999; Hebbecker et al., 2019; Toste et al., 2020; Wang & Guthrie, 2004). However, I need only look back in my own memory to find an illustration of this motivation-thinking relationship.

When I was in elementary school, there was really no such thing as reading comprehension instruction. An inference? What was that? Like many elementary schools at the time, there was a lot of basal readers and answering questions about what happened or writing book reports. But I guarantee you, when I was reading *The Secret Garden* or *Are You There God? It's Me, Margaret*, my mind was doing all the visualizing, predicting, and inferring while reading that are the ingredients in creating a "situation model" experience, that coherent and developed mental representation of the text (Kintsch & van Djik, 1978). This ability to create a mental model, what some teachers call a mind movie, is in fact the very reason why reading is so enjoyable—an experience that certainly predates comprehension instruction.

Describing the high levels of thinking that occurred when I was an 8-year-old reader is not meant to be a statement about whether or not we need comprehension instruction. After all, the development of comprehension instruction is based on the idea that we *can* teach internal reading skills and not do what was standard in my elementary days, which is to continually assess students. Now we understand that we can help young readers better construct mental representations while reading a text through modeling and teaching concepts like visualizing or asking inferential questions. So, yes, inferring is something that can be taught, but we teach it because that is what happens naturally when students experience a deep-level rather than surface-level processing of what they read (Afflerbach et al., 2015).

The purpose of recounting my experience as a young reader is to point out that this powerful role between motivation and constructing mental images is bidirectional. That is, teaching comprehension skills can support engagement in reading but creating situations in which students are motivated to read also supports active use of the comprehension skills we teach. So *in addition* to any comprehension skill modeling, teaching, and guided practice, we will have a better chance of creating a context in which students do this type of desired thinking independently if we attend to the other side of this relationship as well.

DURING TALKING

There are two different ways the talk in HART can support higher-order thinking. The first happens naturally when students are given permission to "share one thing" as opposed to summarizing what they read. There are several hidden, but very intentional, aspects to calling this stage "share one thing." Most obvious perhaps is the word "share," which connotes the natural and social aspect of what we do when we learn interesting information. There is also an implied reciprocity in the word share, meaning it is not a time for one person to explain or tell someone what the text was about, but for an exchange of learning experiences. The use of "thing," although subtle, is also important. This is a general term that encapsulates all types of information and thoughts, from literal recall of information to higher-level thoughts. What drives the "thing" that is shared is based on the relationship between the reader and the text—an experience that is unique to each student. The generalness of "thing" also makes this task accessible for students at all reading levels because it allows for different cognitive entry points. Readers at any place on the motivational continuum can be successful.

Figure 5.1. Students Sharing During Reading

Importantly, this more authentic task of sharing one thing that mirrors what we do as readers in the "real world" which may begin with, but is in no way bounded by, recall of information. Therefore, it allows for growth and expansion, both within a conversation and over time. This concept was demonstrated in the transcript in Chapter 4 when students were talking about the Panama Canal. Because there was no boundary put around the type of talk that was expected, such as when we ask students to summarize, and because the talk was social in nature, this natural movement from students stating a fact about what they learned to thinking about that information occurred easily.

Although this movement from literal to inferential thinking can occur on its own, teachers can and should also intentionally lift up the type of talk that occurs once the steps of HART have become routine. One option for lifting up the kind of talk students do is to explicitly connect it with ongoing comprehension instruction. A common limitation of structured reading curricula is that, while there have been some improvements in the inclusion of informational passages and emphasis on higher-order thinking, most programs rarely reflect a true gradual release of responsibility model that gives space for student-led practice (Dewitz et al., 2009). As such, purposefully linking instruction to formats like HART can give students an authentic and more student-driven context in which to practice the different comprehension strategies that are taught.

You can start each HART session with a reminder about these connections as a way to lift up the way students are reading, writing, or talking. For example, if 5th-graders have been studying visualizing while reading, before students start their HART reading a teacher can say, "Today after you share something interesting you learned from your reading, see if you can say what that information looked like in your mind while you were reading it. What did you visualize?" As will be discussed further in the next chapter, you can also teach an actual minilesson before HART in which you model and teach a comprehension strategy followed by student practice.

Whether giving a reminder or an actual lesson that connects comprehension strategies to the talk they are doing in HART, it is beneficial to model the effort behind this task. In other words, whether it is talking about questions, connections, or theories, students should understand these are not always there at the surface like they might be with fiction. So don't stop at just modeling the actual type of thinking; also model reaching for this information. For example, if I were modeling the concept of asking questions about information with a text about weather, I would ideally not just share a fact about hail and then seamlessly move on to asking an inferential question, but rather first pause and then, while squinting up at the ceiling, say, "Hmmmm . . . " to make visible the effort of thinking. Complementing this type of modeling should be an explicit explanation that when a question or a theory or a connection does not come automatically, it does not mean you say, "Well, there's no connection there." You reach, you make the effort to find that question or connection.

After modeling a type of thinking, you can have students quickly try it out, so they can actively process what you are teaching. This "try it out" phase can be as simple as reading a different paragraph from the same book out loud and then having students do a quick turn-and-talk with a partner about what they learned and a question they could ask about that information (or whatever comprehension strategy you are encouraging). This one-minute turn-and-talk can be followed by a few students sharing with the class. The last part of the lesson should make an explicit connection to the talk they do in HART, for example, saying, "So today during the Read and Share, see if you can do this: after you talk about what you learned, ask a 'why' or a 'why do you think' question about that information." For additional reinforcement you can post this reminder on a screen or a poster. Then, at the end of HART, you can also have a few groups share out questions they asked and then remind students to try to use this same strategy in their reader's notebooks.

Some teachers might prefer to simply replace the "share one thing you learned" with the comprehension strategy directed talk, although I would encourage you not to. Sequencing the thinking from literal to higher order allows students to first recall the information before thinking critically, which has both cognitive and affective implications. While it is true that inferential questions require students to connect a greater amount of text in a more cognitively complex fashion compared to a literal question like "What did you learn?" (Aguiar et al., 2010), recalling learning as a first step creates an important platform, a foundation for the critical thinking you are asking them to do (Hale & Kim, 2020). This two-step expectation also allows all students to be successful, which has important implications for self-efficacy, particularly for students without strong academic self-concepts (Margolis & McCabe, 2004).

Explicit connections to types of critical thinking, of course, do not have to be linked to other types of comprehension strategies you are currently teaching. In fact, a particularly powerful route to expanding the type of talk students do during the "share one thing" is to document and then teach the kinds of thinking that you hear students doing on their own. The next chapter describes how to notice the kinds of talk students do in their teams and use those observations to give immediate feedback via a group conference or a whole-class lesson the next day. Finally, since HART is meant to take the place of traditional independent reading (i.e., it is not meant to take the place of something like a literature circle), teachers looking for additional ways to have students think critically about the informational texts they read for an extended amount of time can follow HART with 10 to 15 minutes of small-group discussion time that has a more explicit focus on higher-order thinking as the primary purpose of talk such as literature circles with roles tailored to informational texts (Barone & Barone, 2016) or other discussion formats such as Questioning the Author (Beck et al., 1997) or Concept Oriented Reading Instruction (Guthrie et al., 2004).

DURING WRITING ABOUT READING

Although reader's notebooks are not part of HART itself, their presence is a critical complement to students' independent reading. Writing about reading is such a powerful vehicle for reading comprehension and critical thinking because it slows down thinking and allows readers to be highly reflective and strategic about their thinking. In a meta-analysis about the impact of writing on reading, Graham and Hebert (2011) offer the following additional reasons why writing about reading is so valuable:

1. It fosters explicitness, as the writer must select which information in text is most important.
2. It is integrative, as it encourages the writer to organize ideas from text into a coherent whole, establishing explicit relationships among the ideas.

3. It facilitates reflection, as the permanence of writing makes it easier to review, reexamine, connect, critique, and construct new understandings of text ideas.
4. It can foster a personal involvement with text, as it requires active decision making about what will be written and how it will be treated.
5. It involves transforming or manipulating the language of text so that writers put ideas into their own words, making them think about what the ideas mean (p. 712).

All this from just a reader's notebook! Of course, the *type* of writing that students actually do in their notebooks matters a great deal. A notebook that has pages and pages of sentences that just describe facts and information learned will certainly reflect some of the outcomes of writing about reading as stated by Graham and Hebert (2011) above. But what writing in a notebook allows students to do, in addition to synthesizing learning, is to develop their critical thinking about information in an external and visible way.

Figure 5.2. Student Writing in a Reader's Notebook

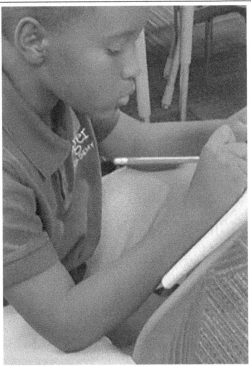

Once students can do HART on their own, you can introduce reader's notebooks (see Appendix A for the lesson). If writing in reader's notebooks is something new in your classroom, I recommend taking a few days to allow students to decorate their notebooks. You can hand out white pieces of paper for them to design and tape on the front and back cover. Covering them with clear contact paper also helps to keep them in good shape. If the notebook is just for HART, you can periodically have students add drawings about information they have learned.

For reader's notebooks, I use the standard marble composition notebooks. I like the line spacing, and they are sturdy enough to withstand the commotion of an elementary classroom and occasional battering from other materials in students' desks (although I prefer students keep all their HART materials in bins separate from their desks). Because I also teach lessons on how to write about your thinking, the front half of their notebook is dedicated to instruction. The second half of the notebook is for independent entries, which is where students write after HART.

Similar to HART itself, the emphasis of writing in reader's notebooks should be on quality over quantity. That is, it is better to have students start out writing for a shorter amount of time, in order to hold up the expectation that it is quality writing time, and then extend the time from there. Not unlike the mechanisms at play in HART, we want to create a habit of mind of high attention writing. I also remind students that after they finish writing, everybody will get a chance to share what they wrote with their teams before we have a public share.

I didn't always have a team share as a consistent part of reader's notebooks. After all, time was short (isn't it always for teachers?), and we only had so many minutes for reader's notebooks as it was, on top of all of the other reading instruction before it was time to move on to math. So, most days, after students wrote, I would jump right from independent writing to the public share where two students read their entries to the class. But, once I started to make room for *all students* to share with each other in their teams, before the whole-class share, I realized creating space for this every time was absolutely worth the trade-off for many reasons.

First, the predictability of sharing with a peer creates an authentic accountability for all students. Similar to the design of HART, which uses the expectation of talk to impact preceding attention, the expectation—the knowledge that you *will soon* be sharing what you are writing—impacts attention while writing. When every student knows that every time after writing in their notebooks, they will share what they wrote with a peer, they are naturally more invested in and give more attention to the task at hand. Additionally, we often remind students to think about "the reader" when writing, either from a craft and mechanics or comprehension standpoint. But unless we create a space for that hypothetical reader to come alive, then the concept does not hold a lot of meaning. Even when students have to turn

Figure 5.3. Students Sharing Reader's Notebook Entries

in work to their teacher, there is a delay in time and space. The audience is not immediate, so it tends to not have as much of an authentic impact on the work itself.

Another benefit of the team share is that students get to hear how someone else processed and thought about the same exact information they just read. By doing this, not only are students exposed to different types of thinking but, because each team writes about the same information, they can more easily relate to and access that thinking. There are also times when students connect with each other when writing about similar reactions or questions. Consider the entries shown in Figure 5.4 and 5.5. Both students are writing what they learned about the brain with some takeaways overlapping.

Creating space for a team share also acknowledges the human desire we have to share with others something we created. While some students may prefer feedback from sharing with the teacher, do not underestimate the satisfaction that comes from students sharing with one another. Making a space in the curriculum for students to facilitate this sharing of work is also one way to develop their social skills within an academic environment (Franklin, 2010).

Figures 5.4 and 5.5. Student Notebook Entries About the Brain

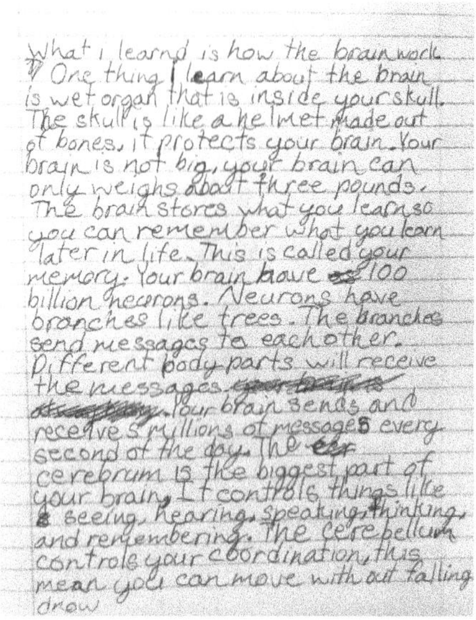

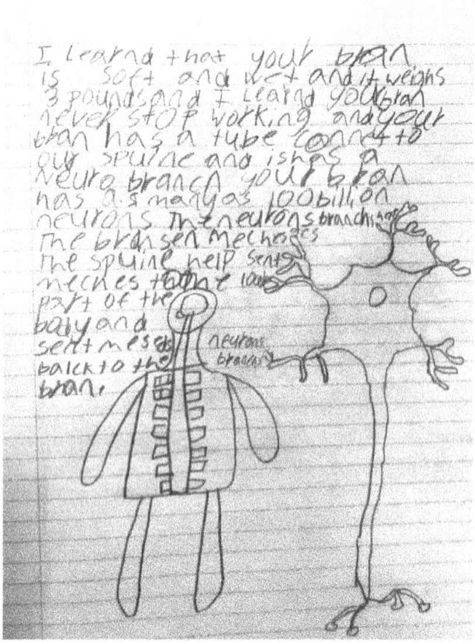

What i learnd is how the brain work. One thing I learn about the brain is wet organ that is inside your skull. The skull is like a helmet made out of bones, it protects your brain. Your brain is not big, your brain can only weighs about three pounds. The brain stores what you learn so you can remember what you learn later in life. This is called your memory. Your brain have 100 billion neurons. Neurons have branches like trees. The branches send messages to each other. Different body parts will receive the messages. Your brain sends and receive 5 myllions of messages every second of the day. The cerebrum is the biggest part of your brain. It controls things like seeing, hearing, speaking, thinking, and remembering. The cerebellum controls your coordination, this mean you can move with out falling draw

I learnd that your brain is soft and wet and it weighs 3 pounds and I learnd you brian never stop working and your brian has a tube connect to our spine and ishes your neuro brain your brian has as many as 100 billion neurons. The neurons branching. The brain sen mechoes. The spuine help sens meckes that that loo part of the bady and sent mesa neurons back to the brach brain.

After students share within their team, you can move on to the public share in which two students, previously chosen, come to the front of the room and read their entries out loud. While students are writing and sharing with each other, be on the lookout for which students you will ask to share with the class, ideally guided by a record of who has already shared. I learned a long time ago that any intention I had of remembering whom I have and have not chosen was just wishful thinking, so I started carrying a clipboard that had every student's name with columns to write the date of when they were chosen to share. As I walk around, I can see at a glance who has not shared in a while.

When notebooks are first introduced, I do take time to teach how this public share is run. The first thing I tell students is that when you come up to share, you need to look around and make sure everyone is looking at you. I tell them that they should expect respect. Regardless of the age of students, I put the ownership of respect on the students. I am always surprised— and love—how much students immediately respond to this responsibility, whether they are in kindergarten or middle school. Perhaps it's the sudden granting of authority, but so many times after I set this expectation, the student who is sharing stands a little taller, scans the room with a regal look, and calls on students who are not paying attention.

After students read their entry, they can call on several peers to comment on their writing or ask questions. At first feedback might relate to the content of their entry or questions and comments about the topic. But after

I have taught lessons on how to bring in thinking to your writing, described briefly below, I start encouraging students to comment on the types of thinking that they hear. Not only does this get students used to listening for types of thinking and not just information, but it also provides ideas for how they might write about information themselves. While giving students the opportunity to write about what they read creates an important opportunity for critical thinking, it doesn't necessarily just happen. The notebook entries above reflect learning about information, which is an important start. But students benefit from lessons and modeling of specific ways to bring thinking into their writing. The next chapter focuses on instruction and illustrates how to teach into students' skill sets for including critical thinking in their entries as they write.

SUPPORTING INDEPENDENCE

As students start doing HART on their own, the role of the teacher shifts: now it is about lifting up the quality of work students do. One way to support independence, once all HART lessons have been taught, is to have a day that focuses on reviewing the steps in HART using the form "Do you have HART?" (shown in Figure 5.6). This form does not have to be done in

Figure 5.6. Do You Have HART? Review Form

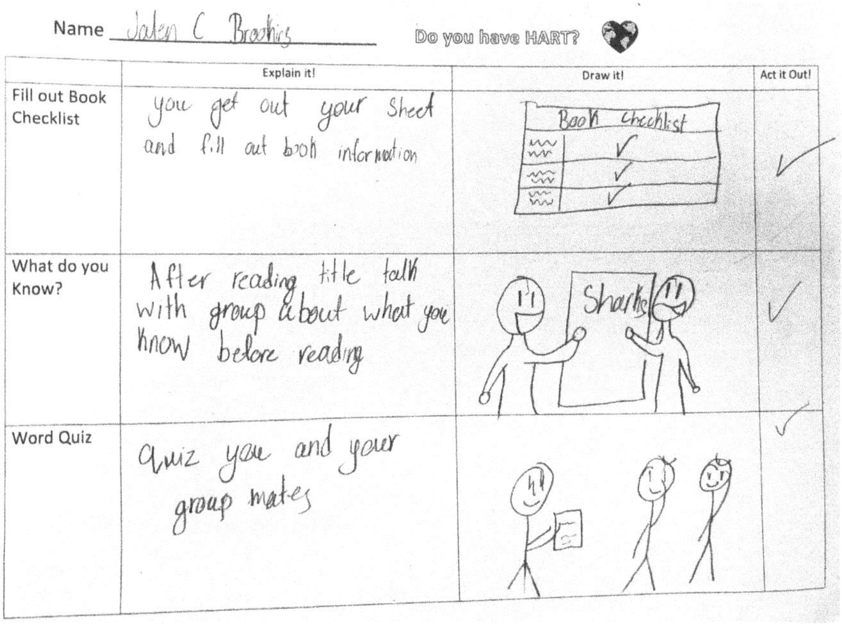

Name Jalen C Brookins

Do you have HART?

	Explain it!	Draw it!	Act it Out!
Fill out Book Checklist	you get out your Sheet and fill out book information	Book checklist ✓ ✓ ✓	✓
What do you Know?	After reading title talk with group about what you know before reading	Sharks	✓
Word Quiz	Quiz you and your group mates		✓

HART teams, but it is designed so that students talk and interact while they fill it out (see Appendix C for a copiable). The different ways of processing and communicating the purpose of each step, through writing, drawing, and acting, create a fun but effective way to solidify students' memory and ownership of each step.

One quick way to support students' independence in bringing critical thinking into their conversations and reader's notebooks is to put up an anchor chart that lists different types of comprehension strategies and related phrases that represent that type of thinking. I often model and have students practice using this type of poster, honing in on the specific skill of being stuck for what to say (or realizing you have only talked or written about what you learned but have not talked about your thinking), turning your head to look at the poster and then getting an idea for either a statement or a question for your group, such as, "Oh yeah! What did you all think about that part we read about bacteria being added to milk to make cheese? What was your reaction?" Or "What did you wonder?" You can also model this same action in relation to reader's notebooks and the idea that if you are not sure what to write about, or feel you have been writing mostly information and what you learned for a while, you can look at this poster to get an idea for what types of thinking you might add. This type of modeling illustrates the idea that if we want students to be independent, it is beneficial to model and practice not just the types of thinking we want them to do but also skills related to initiating those ideas on their own.

Although this type of poster can be useful, students of all levels are more apt to understand and use the types of thinking listed if each one is taught and practiced separately. The next chapter discusses how teachers can support students during HART to lift up the quality of their reading, talking, and thinking through ongoing assessment and responsive instruction in the form of group conferences and minilessons.

CHAPTER 6

Teaching and Assessment

Now that Emma and Leo are a bit older, they have moved on from T-ball. Like the multi-colored Paw Patrol headquarters playset, the T-ball set eventually made its way to the end of our driveway where it was picked up (we assume) by parents of a preschooler ready to start their first lessons on hitting a ball with a bat. Emma and Leo now use oversized plastic bats without any stand for the ball. The fact that they are now independent in hitting balls does not mean, of course, that we are done with feedback. Rarely does one reach independence to never have, or want, feedback again. Think about Major League Baseball (MLB), the highest level of baseball one can reach. Even though those players are the best in the nation, they still get feedback, both in practice and in games. In fact, there are people hired just to give specific types of feedback. Each major league team has pitching coaches, hitting coaches, a third-base coach, a first-base coach, and even a bench coach. And that is not the complete list!

Whether a baseball player is a 6-year-old or an MLB veteran, no one wants *constant* feedback. First of all, it is difficult to incorporate new feedback in a quality way if you do not have time to process the first set of feedback. Second, there is a joy to simply playing without wondering *every time* what someone will say seconds after hitting the ball. Finally, with independence comes a stronger ability to be aware of your own strengths and weaknesses. Despite plenty of support with coaches, MLB players have arguably gotten to where they are because long ago, often pushed by a motivation to improve, they became aware of what aspects of the game they were good at and which ones they needed to improve. This internal feedback is an important part of improving at any skill.

In HART, we want students to experience both the joy and the independence of discussion but, even with MLB players, there is always room to improve. The fact that students are facilitating HART does not mean the role of the teacher is passive: it simply means we move from the role of instructor to coach. In fact, ongoing teacher involvement is essential to the success of HART in your classroom. Yes, the idea is that we have taught lessons so that students can be autonomous in doing HART on their own. But kids are human. Without a sense of accountability from the teacher, conversations have a greater likelihood of devolving into nonbook related topics. But the role of the teacher goes beyond management. Like literature circles, the student-run conversations allow a rich context for us to observe and teach into what students are doing on their own, thereby lifting up the way they talk and think about information.

HART CONFERENCES

This section describes how to use a group conference structure to give students instructional feedback during HART. Group conferences are similar to a typical one-to-one reading conference in that they have a research–decide–teach structure and use current observations of the work students are doing to inform tailor-made teaching (Calkins, 2001). Since discussion is a primary characteristic of HART, group conferences are done during any time students are talking, so during the What Do You Know? Word Quiz, and share time in between independent reading.

When doing the research for these HART conferences, there are three general categories to consider: how students are talking with one another, what they are talking about, and how they are self-managing the HART steps. The first resource I consult is a group's conference sheet (see Table 6.1), a form that lists strengths and teaching points from any previous conferences (see Appendix C for a copiable). If I see that students are demonstrating something I had previously noted they needed to work on, I want to put a spotlight on that when deciding what strength to teach. And if something we talked about last conference is still a clear challenge for them, I would want to seriously consider reinforcing this teaching point.

Then I do what I call my "live" research, which is when I observe and listen in on students' conversations. When I first approach a HART team, I usually sit on the floor next to them, sometimes on a chair. But I don't look at them: I sit with my ear facing the group. I suppose this allows for optimal hearing, but the real reason I do this is that it keeps students' conversation focused on each other. If I watch students while I am listening, many of them often start directing their talk toward me. An additional aspect of my research might include looking at students' book checklists, especially if I have not looked at them for a while.

Table 6.2 presents a number of teaching points you might notice when doing a group conference. These charts are not meant to be a list to pick and choose from each time since your research and your teaching points should be based on observations of *your* students. But I have found that sharing examples of common teaching points offers a good starting point for this kind of conferring and also models the types of specificity that is important for effective feedback. I find that whatever I teach tends to fall in the following categories: the steps in HART, discussion skills, and comprehension

Table 6.1. HART Conference Sheet

HART Team Danielle, Marvin, Mikayla

Date	Strength	Next Step	Notes
10/3	Asking each other — what did you learn — when pause	Use book as a reminder when not sure what else to say.	also — good eye contact
10/9	Word Quiz Each person contributed before read the definition	Start posing questions	
10/16	Asked a "why do you think" question!	Now let question spark a conversation — offer a theory.	maybe teach "maybe" to whole class

skills. The following table lists examples of specific teaching points in each of these three categories.

As should be clear by now, HART has a lot more moving components than traditional independent reading. For some teachers, the picture of 25 students reading quietly at their desks might be more appealing than small groups of students spread out. And, except for the actual independent reading segments, the room is not quiet when HART is happening. But I have long ago learned that rarely is student engagement, and therefore instruction, reaching its potential in a completely quiet classroom. That said, when students are given autonomy, there is always the possibility that a conference, or even a whole-class lesson, will need to focus more on management, and so could be an additional category to consider for group conferences.

Table 6.2. Possible Teaching Points for HART Conferences

Steps in HART

	This might be a STRENGTH if	This might be something to TEACH if
Book Checklists	All students in the group fill out their book checklists accurately and neatly and/or their checklists reflect a range of topic choices.	Not all students in the group fill out their book checklists accurately and neatly and/or their checklists show they are reading mostly about one topic and not a range of topics.
What Do You Know? Using the whole page	When students first choose a book, they use many aspects of the front of the book, such as the title and photographs on the cover to spark discussions about background knowledge.	When students first choose a book, they use only one aspect to spark discussion about background knowledge such as the title.
What Do You Know? Adding what you learned	When doing What Do You Know? students incorporate knowledge they learned from reading their book.	Students think that they should only talk about the cover and not what they learned the day before when reading the book.
Word Quiz Choice	Students look carefully at the text features to choose the appropriate type of Word Quiz.	Students use a type of Word Quiz that does not match the text features in their text.
Word Quiz: It's not about right or wrong	Students make room for different levels of vocabulary knowledge by asking questions like "What do you know about the word...?" or respond positively when someone is not sure of a word but shares where they have heard it.	Students use language that aligns with a right or wrong stance for vocabulary knowledge with phrases such as "What is the correct definition of...?" or when someone offers where they have heard a word before, the Quizzer responds "Wrong! The definition is..."

Table 6.2. (continued)

Discussion Skills

	This might be a STRENGTH if	This might be something to TEACH if
Active Listening	Students are attentive and use eye contact while someone else is sharing an idea.	Students are not using active listening skills while their peers are talking, such as looking at the speaker.
Using the Text for Support	Students consult the book when there is a fact or graphic that they want to talk about but can't recall.	Students talk about information they are not sure about, but do not look back in the text for support.
Asking Questions	Students actively encourage participation from their peers by saying things like "What do you think?" or "What information did you learn?"	Some students actively share ideas, but there are missed opportunities for encouraging participation from others.
Connecting to Ideas	Students actively make connections with their peers with phrases like "I thought the same thing…" or "I had a similar takeaway except I…"	Students describe information they learned, but there is a missed opportunity to be explicit about how what they share connects with what others said.
Making a Circle	Students sit in a way that is physically conducive to having a conversation and making eye contact.	Students sit in a line, at a table, or against a wall, which is keeping them from easily looking at one another when they talk.

Comprehension Skills

	This might be a STRENGTH if	This might be something to TEACH if
Going Beyond a Fact	Students go beyond stating one fact they learned to offer details about that fact.	Students state one fact each, but consistently only say one sentence or offer a surface-level comment.
Connecting to Current Events	Students talk about connections between information from the text and current events.	Students share information but there is a missed opportunity to connect to a current event.

Continued

Table 6.2. (*continued*)

	This might be a STRENGTH if	This might be something to TEACH if
Describing Reactions	After sharing unusual or surprising information, students go on to describe their personal reactions.	After sharing an unusual or surprising fact, students don't share how they felt (amazed, surprised, disgusted, etc.) when they read that fact.
Asking Questions	After sharing learning, students ask wonder questions, such as "Why do you think...?" or a statement that encourages thinking such as "I still don't get why..."	Despite encouraging students to do so in whole-class lessons, students only stick to stating facts but do not pose any questions.
Looking for Networks	Students look for connections between facts that they share, offering analysis of how they connect or work with one another.	Students share facts in a popcorn way where they take turns but do not respond to each other or look for connections.

ENGLISH LEARNERS

If you are working with a group that is comprised of mostly English learners, giving feedback on discussion skills that are grounded in academic language can be particularly beneficial. While language support for nonnative English speakers is ideally an ongoing aspect of instruction, content-area reading offers a unique situation since "as children develop new knowledge, they also need support in using language in new ways" (Schleppegrell, 2012, p. 409). One way to do this is to attend to students' general academic language, that is, terms that are not necessarily related to the content of a book but allow one greater capability in talking about the content of what one reads.

Teaching academic language in a group conference has different repercussions for learning than in a whole-class science lesson when the teacher is typically in charge of conversations because it allows us to teach in an authentic context where the students are in charge. After I offer a teaching point, students try out the language, making their own decisions about when and how to incorporate the language within a natural conversation. There is an immediacy to the application of what I teach, and I am there to give positive or supportive feedback. Also, because I am teaching students as a group, and because they understand by this point that they (not I) facilitate conversations, they can hold each other accountable for the way they talk.

Table 6.3. Possible Language Teaching Points for English Learners

Language Category	Terms or phrases to teach students
Text Features Terms that relate to the different features of informational text	*Glossary* *Table of Contents* *Headings* *Chapters*
Navigating the Text Terms that relate to text features but support students in communicating their use to each other	*If you look at...* *What does the – say?* *I learned this from the...*
Turn Taking Discussion terms that support asking peers to contribute ideas	*What did you learn?* *What do you think about...?"*
Offering Evidence Terms that support stating evidence or asking each other to provide evidence (either background knowledge or information in the text) to support ideas	*I think this because...* *Like it says on page...* *What makes you say that...?* *Where is the text ...?*

Table 6.3 presents different categories of language that can be considered as teaching points when you are having a conference with English learners as well as native speakers who need extra support for discussion skills. For each category, I suggest terms or phrases listed in order of complexity. Once students outgrow these teaching points, you can consider discussion skills such as those listed in Table 6.2

The other aspect of HART to research when having a conference with ELs is to observe how they are using their list of content-related vocabulary words, a section described in Chapter 1. You might notice, for example, students consulting this list when trying to remember the English word for "planet," and so decide to highlight this as a strength in your conference. On the flip side, you might notice that a group of students wrote down vocabulary words for the first book but did not continue the practice when they started reading a new book, in which case this could be a teaching point.

TEACHING STRENGTHS

Once you have researched the way your students are talking and considered both strengths and needs from any of the categories described above, you decide which strength and which teaching point to make public with that group. Regardless of whether I am conferring in reading, writing, or the specific context of HART, my conferences always reflect a symmetry of teaching each student (or group of students) a strength and a next step. Notice I use the phrase *teaching* a strength. This is an intentional choice of words, as it purposely does more than simply give a compliment. Positive feedback or effort praise is always a good thing regardless of what form it comes in. Especially for struggling students, teaching students specifically what they do well and why it is important can have implications for a critical aspect of school success: students' academic self-perception (Hale, 2018).

With HART conferences, once I have decided what strength and next step I want to teach, I pause the group, an interruption they know is followed by feedback. There are two main parts to teaching the strength: naming a specific skill and then saying why it is important. Specificity here matters. I can say things like "Great job sharing what you learned," or "You all are doing a great job with the Word Quiz." As stated before, there is nothing wrong with positive feedback of any kind, but general feedback is a missed opportunity. Not only is specific feedback more informative and so more likely to reinforce desired behaviors, but it carries with it evidence, and so it more strongly contributes to feelings of competence (Chalk & Bizo, 2004; Simonsen et al., 2010). As shown in Table 6.4, you can also reinforce students' understanding of what they are doing well and their confidence by comparing what they are doing to what "other kids" or "some kids" do. Such statements are accurate, but they are also hypothetical. I am not comparing them with anyone in particular. But what this comparison does (and this is particularly important for below–grade-level students or students who are not as academically confident as their peers) is create feelings of competence and capability by putting them on the opposite end of the comparison spectrum from where they are typically used to being, either due to their own perception or grade-level assessments (Hale, 2014).

In any conference I also describe why a particular skill is important; a step that has become a consistent part of my instruction, whether I am teaching a whole-class lesson, a small-group lesson, or a conference. We do this "giving the why" naturally outside the classroom. Just yesterday when Emma was hitting baseballs in the back yard, I noticed she would often swing the bat not sideways but kind of up and over, almost like she was serving a tennis ball. So (after not saying something until I noticed it was pattern) I paused and said, "Emma you want to swing like this, sideways, not down . . ." showing her what I meant with my own invisible bat. "Because you want the ball to go out and if you hit it up and over it will go down to the ground." A simple explanation of course but telling Emma "the why" behind her swing goes beyond the idea of following my direction because "I said so" to supporting her understanding of my feedback, that is her knowledge between her swing and how it affects the ball.

So no matter what skill I teach in a conference, whether it is associated with a strength or something an individual or group needs to work on, I give the why—how does this particular skill help their reading, critical thinking, or discussion skills. Sometimes thinking about the why takes some time: we know it's important, for example, for students to listen to each other. In fact, it is an expectation that perhaps has become so commonplace it seems like an explanation itself. But thinking one more step to how you can communicate the reason behind this expectation adds strength to your teaching and conferring. We can explain that it's important to look at each other when discussing a topic because "it shows respect for someone who is sharing ideas. Can you imagine talking to your friends about what you did over the weekend but they are just looking up at the sky or looking through their pockets? We kind of know they are not paying attention to what we are saying and it doesn't feel good. Plus, when you look at someone while they are talking, you really capture what they're saying, which gives you more to think and talk about in return." Table 6.4 shows examples of some of the teaching points above with this two-part characteristic of naming the strength followed by the why.

The language you use when moving on to address skills a team can work on is similar because you still want them to understand (a) the specific skill you are talking about and (b) why it is important. But since the teaching phase has to do with an aspect of HART that they could improve, there is also an added stage of practice. While you could just have students repeat back to you what they could work on, feedback is much more likely to lead to student ownership if they first practice what you are teaching. If the teaching point is specific, students typically can easily incorporate it during this

Table 6.4. Teaching Strengths With the Why in HART Conferences

HART Steps

Specific Teaching Point	What Am I Teaching?	Why Is It Important?
What Do You Know? Using the whole page	Can I stop you for a second? So one thing you are doing well is that you are using different parts of the cover to talk about what you already know about coral reefs. Some groups might just stick to the title, but you are using some of the detailed photographs on the cover in addition to the words.	That's important because while it's good to talk about the overall topic of coral reefs, the cover includes pictures that give clues about what will be in the book. By noticing the sea urchins and the sea turtle in the corner and talking about what you already know about those things, you are retrieving even more information from way back in your brain related to what you are about to read.

Continued

Table 6.4. (continued)

Discussion Skills

Specific Teaching Point	What Am I Teaching?	Why Is It Important?
Connecting to Ideas	One thing I noticed when you were sharing what you learned is that you made connections between your ideas. I noticed you told Ali "I thought kind of the same thing about the supreme court" before you shared what you learned.	This is great because it means not only are you actively listening to others, but you are also aware of looking at how your ideas connect, or in some cases how they are different. Some groups are just saying what they learned, but are not having a discussion. But it's when we look for how our ideas are similar or different, like you all are, that we can think more deeply about what we are learning.

Comprehension Skills

Specific Teaching Point	What Am I Teaching?	Why Is It Important?
Posing Questions	Can I stop you for a second? I noticed that when you were sharing what you learned you asked a great question, "Why do you think the owls spit out a pellet like that?" I know I taught this idea of asking questions last week, but not everyone is actually doing it on their own yet. I didn't remind you to ask questions, right? You did it totally on your own. That means you are starting to be independent in not just talking about what you learned, but also thinking about this information.	This is important, because these types of wonder questions help us think more deeply about what we learn. There is so much about these topics that are mysteries. Once you start asking each other thoughtful questions, it can really help move the conversation from reviewing and restating information to a much deeper level of thinking.

practice. After they try it out, you can give positive feedback about how they did or, if they had trouble, redirect them and have them try it again.

Table 6.5 shows how the teaching points highlighted in Table 6.4, taught as strengths, might sound like skills students need to work on. Notice how the language of describing the *why* stays largely the same.

Table 6.5. Teaching Guided Practice in HART Conferences

Category	Specific Teaching Point	What Am I Teaching?	Why Is It Important?	Guided Practice
HART Steps	What Do You Know: Using the whole page	Before you move on to the Word Quiz, look at the cover of the book and find some details to discuss.	That's important because while it's good to talk about the overall topic of coral reefs, chances are there are other things on the cover, the sea turtles in the corner or sea urchins, that are also in the book. And by talking about what you already know about those things, you are retrieving even more information from way back in your brain related to what you are about to read.	So why don't you give that a try? Take a few seconds to look at all the details in the photographs on the cover. Then see if you can ask each other what you already know about that?

Continued

Table 6.5. (continued)

Category	Specific Teaching Point	What Am I Teaching?	Why Is It Important?	Guided Practice
Discussion Skills	Connecting to Ideas	One thing I notice when you are sharing what you learned is that you are going around a circle, kind of like popcorning your learning and then going right back to the book. You're saying great things about what you learned, but one thing you can work on is making this more of a discussion. And one way you can do that is by being aware of how your learning or ideas connect to one another, or how they are different. You can use phrases like "I thought the same thing…" You can even give feedback like, "Yeah that was a cool fact."	This is important because when you can connect or give feedback to another person, it means you are actively listening to that person. Also, when we consider how our ideas are similar or different from some one else's, we can think more deeply about what we are learning.	So go ahead and read your next section. This time, when you share what you learned, look for ways to connect with what someone else says, even if it's sharing a reaction.
Comprehension Skills	Posing Questions	You are doing a great job sharing your learning, but one thing you can start working on is to talk about what you think about that information. One way to do that is, after you share something you learned, pose a Why or How question related to that information.	These types of wonder questions help us think more deeply about what we learned. And it can just lead to more interesting conversations! Remember sometimes looking for these questions takes effort. But once we find one, it can really help move the conversation to a deeper place where you're not just restating facts.	When it's time to share, I will come back over and listen in. After you share something you learned, I would like one of you to ask a Why or How question about that information. It doesn't have to be about your information—you can ask a question that relates to what someone else in your group shared.

The last thing I do at the end of a group conference is have students repeat the teaching points back to me, both their strength and what they worked on. I learned a long time ago that head nodding when I ask students questions like "Does that make sense?" or "Do you understand?" means very little. Not only does repeating the teaching points back to me let *me* know they know, but going through the extra effort of having to verbalize what they are good at and what they need to work on can further solidify learning for the students. One option at this point is for students to record their own teaching points in a section of their reader's notebook. Although this extra step extends the time away from their HART work, it can be a helpful scaffold for those students who might benefit from additional accountability. Once students move on to their reader's notebooks, you can continue with individual conferences but now with a shift to supporting the way students are bringing thinking into their writing.

Finally, regardless of what you decide to teach in these HART conferences, it is critical to record the teaching points. Writing down what I teach creates a greater sense of accountability for the students, but it also keeps *me* accountable for actually teaching something and not just "checking in" with a group (Hale, 2008). Additionally, unless you write down what you teach, you cannot use it as a resource the next time you meet with a team. Record keeping does not need to be complex. In fact, if my teaching is specific, writing down what I taught can often be summed up in a phrase. (See Table 6.1 for an example). Since being a teacher requires far too many pieces of white paper, I find it helpful to keep these in a colored binder, so when it's time for HART I can just grab it and go.

Similar to any independent reading, incorporating one-on-one reading conferences into your daily schedule provides Tier 3 instruction that allows you to give tailor-made teaching to your students (Berne & Degener, 2015), which is something you can still do in HART. Most of this chapter focuses on the lesser known practice of group conferences, but when students are doing their silent independent reading, I strongly encourage doing individual conferences, especially with students who are reading below grade level and need that extra support. Since the time that students are reading is in shorter segments, especially when HART is new, you can do what Lucy Calkins (2001) calls a coaching conference, where the teacher is not having a formal one-to-one conversation and instruction time but instead quickly listens to the students read and offers light instructional touches, some reminders or nudges where a need is observed. These check-in conferences are valuable not only because they give in-the-moment individual support but also because you can get to many more students, giving the expectation of high attention reading an additional layer of accountability.

MINILESSONS

Anything you notice as a pattern in the way students are reading, writing, or talking during HART can be addressed in a minilesson either before or after students get into their teams. The skills listed in Table 6.5, for example, if they are applicable to many students and not just one group, could all be possible lesson topics. I should clarify that when I say minilesson in this context, I really do mean *mini*. Unlike a reader's notebook or writing workshop minilesson that might involve substantial student practice and last 20 minutes, minilessons in HART are meant to be only 5 to 10 minutes. Remember HART is not about instruction but is a temporary scaffolding for independent reading. That said, an abbreviated lesson can be an effective way to address whole-class patterns.

If, for example, during What Do You Know? I noticed a number of groups are having a hard time remembering what they read the previous time, especially if it's a Monday or has been a few days since HART, I can use a lesson to show students how they can briefly look in their book or their reader's notebook for a few seconds for a refresher and then close it again, emphasizing that while we want to recall information mostly from our brains, looking back to what we read or wrote before can be helpful in reminding us of what we learned. You can also model the thinking behind the action, by saying out loud, "What was it we read last time?" opening to a page, scanning briefly, and then closing the book, saying, "Oh yeah! I remember that the U.S. Mint makes billions of coins every year but it's not up to them how many to make." Lessons, even if brief, should also include the Why. In this example, I remind students that what they learned last time is already in their head somewhere, but sometimes just seeing a visual or a phrase can pop it back to the front of their mind. Then you can do a quick turn and talk and say, "Tell someone next to you, what can you do if it's time for What Do You Know? and you are having a hard time remembering information?"

READER'S NOTEBOOK LESSONS

The idea of encouraging students to write about their thinking in their reader's notebooks is not a new one. When I first started teaching 20 years ago, I remember seeing a sudden influx of posters that said "Reading Is Thinking" and students being taught what an inference was. Teaching reading comprehension (and not just assessing it) was an important shift in reading instruction. But I found that a lot of the comprehension instruction and scaffolding that was happening in the rug area during read-alouds, guided reading, or whole-class lessons on inferring or predicting was not really transferring to students' notebook entries, at least not in their independent entries.

In a way, this made sense since with most comprehension instruction, students were not the initiators of the thinking. The skill of autonomously incorporating thinking as you write, or as you talk for that matter, about a story or information is a unique skill that necessitates instruction targeted to that task (Hale, 2014). Cognitively there is a huge gap between being able to recite what it means to infer or answering an inferential question and being able to produce this type of thinking on your own without a prompt. Therefore, *in addition* to modeling and teaching comprehension skills, we can also teach students specific ways they can incorporate critical thinking in their writing.

Extending beyond writing about what you learned does not always come naturally. Very often if students are new to reader's notebooks, I first work on expanding and developing the way they write about what they learned. Modeling a before-and-after example on a screen can be a helpful way to illustrate the difference with your first example showing a list of facts and second example showing paragraphs that include detailed information about a topic before moving onto the next "fact." Focusing first on developing students' descriptions of what they learn provides a stronger foundation of material and information before emphasizing or even explicitly teaching students how to think critically in their reader's notebook entries.

One way we can do this is to teach students the language of thinking. In *Readers Writing* (Hale, 2014), I describe how teaching students specific language that falls under more general categories of comprehension skills, such as analyzing or synthesizing, make these sometimes nebulous concepts more tangible, which means students are more likely to incorporate them into writing on their own. Rather than just teach the concept of critical thinking, we can also teach "one small way" to do a certain type of critical thinking through writing. My favorite example of this "teaching the small parts of critical thinking" is the word *maybe*. The very nature of this word implies inferential thinking because we use it when we are not sure, but have some evidence to make us think something. In my literacy course, for example, I explain we would not say, "Maybe today is Wednesday," or "Maybe we are in room 1260." These are facts. "But," I pose to my students, "What if 9:00 has come and gone, it's now 9:30, and I have still not shown up for class. What might you think?" One student suggests, "Maybe one of your kids is sick." Another student says, "Or maybe you got stuck in traffic." I point out how they used their background knowledge of me (I am a mother of three small children) or their knowledge of Jacksonville (there can be a lot of traffic on the many bridges and highways that lead to the University of North Florida) to make a theory of why I would not be there.

Teaching the word "maybe" is based on the premise that, rather than just model, teach, and have students practice the concept of inferring and hope for language that reflects that type of thinking to appear in their notebook entries or in their conversations, we can actually teach specific language that goes along with this type of thinking. This teaching the language

Figure 6.1. Student Notebook Entry About Shells

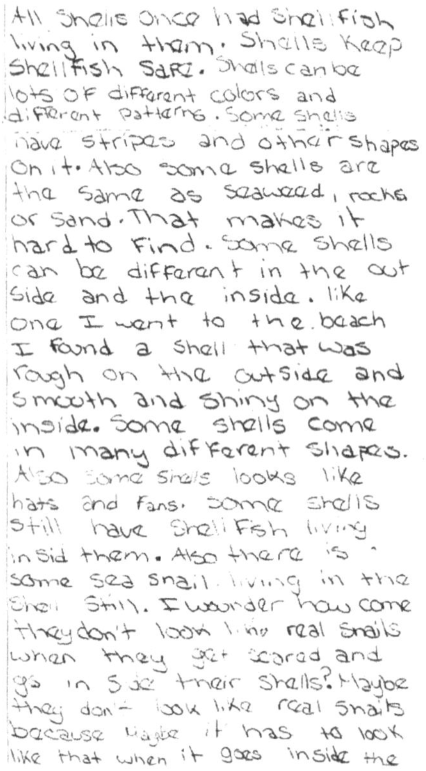

> All Shells once had Shell Fish
> living in them. Shells keep
> Shellfish safe. Shells can be
> lots of different colors and
> different patterns. Some shells
> have stripes and other shapes
> on it. Also some shells are
> the same as seaweed, rocks
> or sand. That makes it
> hard to find. Some Shells
> can be different in the out
> side and the inside. Like
> one I went to the beach
> I found a shell that was
> rough on the outside and
> smooth and shiny on the
> inside. Some shells come
> in many different shapes.
> Also some shells looks like
> hats and fans. Some shells
> still have shell Fish living
> insid them. Also there is
> some sea snail living in the
> shell still. I wonder how come
> they don't look like real snails
> when they get scared and
> go in sid their shells? Maybe
> they don't look like real snails
> because maybe it has to look
> like that when it goes inside the

of thinking is particularly beneficial for English learners who often need to learn the academic language that goes along with different disciplines. In their writing on the challenges of academic language, Snow and Uccelli (2009) highlight the idea that academic language can be seen as a continuum; that there is no particular level or complexity of language use that makes it suddenly *academic*. The word *maybe* is a great example of a word that, while widely used and not very complex, is nevertheless a vehicle for the types of critical thinking we want students to do. Table 6.6 shows examples of other lessons that show students one specific way to incorporate a type of thinking into students' writing.

Oral language, of course, is the foundation for any writing we do. Therefore, any lesson on bringing critical thinking into writing will be far more effective if we, at the same time, encourage students to also bring this type of thinking into their talk about texts. Since HART includes time for both student-led discussions and reader's notebooks, it offers the perfect opportunity for this dual emphasize of spoken and written language. With the above lesson on the word *maybe* as a vehicle for thinking inferentially, for

Table 6.6. Sample Lesson Topics for Writing About Reading

Strategy Lesson	Related Comprehension Skill	What It Is	Why Is It Important?
All My Senses	Visualizing	Using other senses besides sight when describing a mind movie, using phrases like "I could smell…" or "I could hear."	Helps to bring alive the information that you are writing about.
World Connections	Connections	Making connections between information learned and current events, using phrases like "That makes me think of…"	Connects two sets of background knowledge to inform each other.
Explaining your Question	Questioning/ Analyzing	After asking a question, write at least two sentences that further explain what this question is about.	Brings in knowledge you *do* know and makes you more aware of what exactly it is that you wonder or question.
Maybe Theories	Inferring	After asking a question, offer a theory in response to this question starting with the word *Maybe*.	Helps the question lead to critical thinking that draws on learned knowledge.

Lesson Topics from *Readers Writing: Lessons for Responding to Narrative and Informational Text* (Hale, 2014)

example, my minilesson would first be directed to students' talk before they start HART that day. For the try-it-out part I can read a paragraph out loud, ask someone to offer a wonder question (or just give my own), and then have students turn and talk to see if they can offer a theory with the word *maybe*. Then, after a brief class share, I would encourage students to use this language when they talk in their groups by saying, "So today, when you talk about what you have learned, see if you can ask some wonder questions and use this word *maybe* to try and offer some theories."

Later on in HART, just before students are about to write in their reader's notebooks, I would take one minute to remind everyone to try to use this same thinking language in their entries. Then, in the whole-class share, I would choose at least one student who used this type of thinking in their entry. To reinforce ownership and continued use of this strategy, you can also add this language to the independence anchor chart described at the end of

Chapter 5 that offers students support for independently adding thinking into their talking and writing.

ASSESSING HART

Because HART is meant to support independent reading, any related assessments need to match the purpose of HART. The following rubric (Table 6.7) can be used every few weeks or once a month to capture how students are doing with the different expectations of HART, such as organization of materials, genre choices, the management and facilitation of discussions, and students' notebooks. After introducing the rubric, you can let students know that in a few weeks, instead of doing your regular conferences, you will take a few days to go to each group, observe their materials, and watch them in action for a few minutes to formally assess them with this rubric. Remind them that, since HART is done as a group, everyone in the group receives the same score. To make the rubric even more meaningful, you can have students fill it out as a self-assessment first and keep it in their folder.

Table 6.7. HART Assessment Rubric

Group _____   Date _____

	Not Visible	Needs Improvement	Yes, Doing a Good Job!	Notes
Choosing books on your level				
Book list filled out correctly				
Reading a range of topics				
Doing all steps in HART				
Notebooks reflect time given for writing				
Entries include information and thinking				

Notice these expectations are doable by all levels of students and are not about grade-level standards. Grade-level expectations are of course important. Not having them in the HART rubric is not about diluting high expectations. Quite the opposite. When all students are capable of meeting expectations, I can hold everyone accountable for a high level of work. This expectation also means students, especially those who are not strong academically, are more likely to take it seriously. For example, if notebook entries were graded on whether I think they match what a 5th- or 8th-grade student *should* be able to produce or how students wrote compared to their peers, why would my students who read and write below grade level and likely already have some resistance to writing try hard? But the expectation that everyone is writing entries that reflect the amount of time given supports the very idea of differentiation, that writing to one's potential looks different for different students. I can also hold all levels of students accountable for including both factual information (what I learned) and some thinking about that information.

Incorporating conferring and instruction around HART is not always easy: it requires time, energy, and additional management of materials. Once students know how to do HART and are autonomous in carrying on productive conversations during What Do You Know?, Word Quiz, and in between independent reading, it can be tempting to focus just on being the timekeeper or keeping a management eye on groups. After all, the beauty of HART is that the students are the ones facilitating discussions. But this independent work is not just a goal; it is also a valuable vehicle through which you can lift up the skills and strategy use of your students. By continuously assessing (formally and informally) the work that goes on in HART and then offering responsive support and instruction (both in lesson and conferences), teachers can greatly impact the level of reading, writing, and talking students do during this time, both as independent readers and collaborative critical thinkers.

CHAPTER 7

Content Area Reading

One of the paradoxes of teaching is that, despite how much time we spend every school day on teaching and learning, there never seems to be enough of it. Elementary teachers are responsible for so many subjects—reading, writing, math, vocabulary, and often science and social studies—and teaching them well. And while middle school and high school teachers are not responsible for so many different subjects, the number of students they teach quadruples. The time we spend planning for and actually teaching does not even take into account all the other things that happen throughout a school week: calls and conferences with parents, IEP meetings, planning field trips, and giving assessments, just to name a few. And, of course, all this often has to be done within the confines of whatever curriculum our school or district has deemed best for our students as well as the many state standards. In a nutshell, time in a school day is precious.

CONNECTIONS TO STANDARDS

One of the greatest benefits of HART is that it addresses a number of academic targets at the same time within several disciplines: reading, writing, social studies, science, and vocabulary. As shown in Table 7.1, because HART involves discussion and writing in addition to reading, there are multiple literacy skills addressed. Some of these skills are more directly supported by HART, such as the use of text features to navigate and comprehend text. Others, such as the mechanics of writing, are not necessarily a targeted skill of HART but are still things students need to call on when writing in their reader's notebooks. Table 7.1 also illustrates how each component aligns with the standards set forth by the Common Core. HART directly reflects some of these standards while, for others, HART is an opportunity to address these standards. For example, if students are doing HART in a 5th-grade classroom, some groups may naturally exhibit standard RI.5.3 about examining relationships between two concepts in a text in their discussions. But you can also explicitly address and teach students this skill using either a minilesson or conference as described in Chapter 6. The same is true for some of the writing standards. Some students may use phrases such as *however* or *in contrast* naturally when writing about information

Table 7.1. Alignment Between HART Components and Literacy Skills and Standards

HART	Literacy Skills	CCSS Alignment
Reading Short increments of high attention reading	Fluency with informational text	CCSS.ELA-LITERACY.RI.5.1 Quote accurately from a text when explaining what the text says explicitly and when drawing inferences from the text
Authentic talk about text read	Reading stamina	
	Literal and inferential comprehension	CCSS.ELA-LITERACY.RI.5.3 Explain the relationships or interactions between two or more individuals, events, ideas, or concepts in a historical, scientific, or technical text based on specific information in the text
Interaction with text features as part of Word Quiz	Awareness of text features	
		CCSS.ELA-LITERACY.RI.5.6 Analyze multiple accounts of the same event or topic, noting important similarities and differences in the point of view they represent

	HART	Literacy Skills	CCSS Alignment
Writing	Reader's notebook entries that focus on a combination of information learned and thinking	Recall and synthesis of information	CCSS.ELA-LITERACY.W.5.2 Write informative/explanatory texts to examine a topic and convey ideas and information clearly
		Incorporating critical thinking about information	CCSS.ELA-LITERACY.W.5.2.B Develop the topic with facts, definitions, concrete details, quotations, or other information and examples related to the topic
		Mechanics and grammar of writing	CCSS.ELA-LITERACY.W.5.2.C Link ideas within and across categories of information using words, phrases, and clauses (e.g., *in contrast, especially*)
			CCSS.ELA-LITERACY.W.5.9 Draw evidence from literary or informational texts to support analysis, reflection, and research
Vocabulary	Attention to vocabulary supports in text including Glossary, word lists and bolded content words	Content related vocabulary	CCSS.ELA-LITERACY.SL.5.6 Adapt speech to a variety of contexts and tasks, using formal English when appropriate to task and situation
		Academic language	
	Student-driven discussion of word knowledge related to content topics	Expressive and receptive vocabulary	CCSS.ELA-LITERACY.RI.5.4 Determine the meaning of general academic and domain-specific words and phrases in a text

Continued

Table 7.1. (*continued*)

	HART	Literacy Skills	CCSS Alignment
Science and Social Studies	Reading, writing, and talking about social studies and science topics	Wide reading of content topics	CCSS.ELA-LITERACY.RI.5.10 By the end of the year, read and comprehend informational texts, including history/social studies, science, and technical texts, at the high end of the grades 4–5 text complexity band independently and proficiently
	Sharing and listening to peer's topics during reader's notebook share	Growing familiarity with informational text	
		Social and authentic context for discussing content topics	CCSS.ELA-LITERACY.RI.5.6 Analyze multiple accounts of the same event or topic, noting important similarities and differences in the point of view they represent
			Also see Grades 6–8 ELA Standards for History/Social Studies and Science & Technical Subjects

	HART	Literacy Skills	CCSS Alignment
Discussion: **Speaking** **and** **Listening**	Authentic and student-driven talk about texts read	Use of discussion phrases	CCSS.ELA-LITERACY.SL.5.1 Engage effectively in a range of collaborative discussions (one-on-one, in groups, and teacher-led) with diverse partners on grade 5 topics and texts, building on others' ideas and expressing their own clearly
		Expressive and receptive vocabulary	
		Accountability for comprehension	CCSS.ELA-LITERACY.SL.5.1.A Come to discussions prepared, having read or studied required material; explicitly draw on that preparation and other information known about the topic to explore ideas under discussion
		Discussion norms: eye contact, listening, and responding to peers	
			CCSS.ELA-LITERACY.SL.5.1.B Follow agreed-upon rules for discussions and carry out assigned roles
			CCSS.ELA-LITERACY.SL.5.1.C Pose and respond to specific questions by making comments that contribute to the discussion and elaborate on the remarks of others

but you can also teach the use of certain academic language in short lessons or even conferences. Although the standards listed in this table are for 5th grade, they are applicable to grades both above and below.

While the alignment to literacy standards, whether Common Core or otherwise, are important, both in theory and for teachers to be able to verbalize how time taken from the day to do something like HART is a valuable use of time, any teacher knows that what matters just as much is the level with which students are engaged with any given task. I can create worksheets or plan a whole-class lesson that "addresses the standards," but if it is the 5th worksheet that feels like busy work or it is a lesson in which only my top readers can genuinely participate, then how effective or valuable is it? The standards can be helpful in terms of planning, but in order for them to support meaningful instruction we have to consider how *all* our students apply this standard and do so actively, not passively.

CONNECTIONS TO CURRICULUM

Another benefit of HART is that it addresses, and is meant to temporarily replace, an element that just about every reading program supports: independent reading. Therefore, once students learn how to do it, HART can be incorporated into the school day and week in a variety of ways regardless of whether there is a structured reading curriculum or not. A 4th-grade teacher who is not bound by a district reading curriculum, for example, might decide to begin HART in November as part of a nonfiction unit of study. Within his reading block, he might have whole-class lessons, read-alouds, and guided reading to support students' ability to read and think about informational text. But independent reading and reader's notebooks could be done within the HART framework. His students might do HART until February, during which time he is building students' stamina as described in Chapter 4, so that when he returns to more traditional independent reading, where students are reading a variety of genre, they have improved how they read informational text on their own (and their enthusiasm for this genre). A 5th-grade teacher in another district with a highly structured reading program, however, may not have as much flexibility. But since independent reading is an expected part of the curriculum, she can still incorporate HART. After taking a few weeks in October to teach the HART lessons, she might have a schedule so that 3 days during the reading block students do traditional independent reading and the other 2 days they do HART.

These different schedules reflect the idea that scaffolding for reading informational text can be seen from two different perspectives: one from within your own grade and one from the point of view of the students and their K–12 experience. By using HART in the months of November, December and January, the first teacher is scaffolding students for the way they read informational texts once they return to traditional independent reading in February. In the 5th-grade class, there may not be an exact transition from one type of reading to another, but it is still scaffolding because it has implications for the skills and habits of mind students bring with them to the next grade. While many might agree with this last sentence, it is important to highlight the hidden message, which is that scaffolding is not just about what happens within your own grade while students are in your view. Reading this genre at a high level is a skill that takes a long time to develop and is certainly not mastered in one year, especially as the texts themselves become more complex.

One way to incorporate HART in the primary grades is to use a version called "HART Junior" that uses read-alouds in addition to independent reading. As shown in Table 7.2, this version has the same steps as HART except some of the reading is done by the teacher (see Appendix C for a copiable version of the steps for HART Junior). Although a main purpose of HART is to create conditions of high attention independent reading, an equally important goal is supporting wide reading and content knowledge development. Additionally, even though students are not doing the reading themselves, the intermittent peer talk and anticipation of that talk can still impact heightened attention and comprehension, just through aural means. Any elementary school that uses HART in the upper grades or in their after-school program will also benefit if younger students come used to this format of reading and discussion.

To further enrich HART Junior, teachers can create units such that 2 or 3 days that use the reading format shown in Table 7.2 are followed by 1 or 2 days when students read sets of guided reading books about the same topic using the standard HART format. Since reading at this age is still sometimes an external rather than internal activity, teachers can opt to have students do pair reading where students take turns reading aloud the pages of text while the other person monitors, meaning they follow along and offer any support, such as pointing out where meaning might be found in a picture or, after some wait time, offering the first letter sound of a word. Students still alternate between reading and sharing with an emphasis on talking about information embedded in the illustrations as well as what they read. Then, in their reader's notebook or folders, they would add on to their previous entry. Primary teachers can also end these units by doing a fiction read aloud, both to strengthen the application of knowledge learned but also to make connections between genres.

One example of this type of HART Junior unit that Read USA uses with 2nd-graders is on snow. Teachers first read *Curious about Snow*, a nonfiction read aloud, for several days using the format shown in Table 7.2. Then students have two days where they use HART to read a level G guided reading book about blizzards in pairs. On the final day, teachers read *The Snowy Day* by Ezra Jack Keats with specific comprehension questions

Table 7.2. HART Junior

HART Component	Description	Suggested Time Frame
What Do You Know?	Before reading, ask students to turn and talk about what they know about this topic or what they remember from last time. Then have several students share out with the class.	2–3 minutes
Word Quiz	Choose three content vocabulary words from the book (the Glossary, Word List or text). Words can be from upcoming pages or from pages they already read. For each word, show what it looks like on an index card or sentence strip and then have students turn and talk and ask each other: "What do you know about the word…?" Have several students share after each word and offer the definition if needed.	5 minutes
Read and Share	Read short segments of the read aloud. After each segment have students turn to each other and talk about something they learned. Repeat this "Read and Share" format at least three times. Remind students that they will be able to draw and write what they talked about afterwards. (Once students understand how to do HART Jr., you can start encouraging different types of thinking during the share time).	10–15 minutes
Reader's Notebooks or Folders	Students go back to their desks or tables to draw, label, and write about the information they remember from the read aloud and their conversations. At the end, students share what they drew and wrote with each other followed by a whole-class share.	10–15 minutes

to encourage both higher-order thinking such as "Why do you think Peter dreamt the snow melted?" and questions specifically targeted to the application of knowledge from the unit such as "What didn't Peter understand about snow when he put the snowball in his pocket?"

Because HART targets reading of informational text, it can also be used in middle and high school grades within content area subjects. Science and social studies teachers can use this format to supplement and complement direct instruction. For example, a 7th-grade teacher who is teaching a unit on oceans and geology might primarily use the district-provided science textbook. Instead of having students read sections of the text on their own (or having one student read aloud while others follow along, which creates an active reading experience for only one student), she could have students read sections of the textbook using HART, including the What Do You Know? and Word Quiz steps. Since the aspect of matching texts to readers is absent, teachers may want to use heterogenous grouping rather than similar ability groups to offer additional support for below–grade-level and English learner readers.

Another option is for content area teachers to create a small HART library with sets of books that reflect topics covered throughout the year and have students do HART once or twice a week. As mentioned previously, an important feature of content knowledge development is that it occurs not by accumulating isolated facts, but by expanding and deepening one's schema of interrelated sets of information or concept networks (Fitzgerald et al., 2017). Complementing direct instruction about a primary topic with time for students to read and talk about related topics not only adds variety to the learning formats and opportunities for engaging students but also expands contributing networks of knowledge. For example, a social studies teacher whose curriculum focuses on the economy and the national banking system could have sets of books in her HART library about those specific topics but also sets of books about currency exchange, the stock market, real estate and the housing market, the history of money, and international currency exchanges. This teacher can have groups of students write about and then present on their topics to the class with the added expectation that they explain how information they learned relates to the main topic of study. This type of "expert" contribution from students multiplies the content networks to which students are exposed, but also impacts students' engagement and sense of efficacy.

CONNECTIONS TO TESTING

Running underneath HART and other discussion-oriented reading formats is the idea that preparing students to be the best readers they can be requires us to address the affective side of reading. How students experience reading and view themselves as readers matters greatly for the level of effort and internal work they are willing to do. This statement is not just about reading: it's about the human condition. If my twins went to a baseball camp, yes, I would expect some drills and some coaching and feedback. But one of the main goals of the camp, one would hope, is that students have lots of time to play the game with each other and come away liking to play baseball. What better foundation can you have for young baseball players than for them to love the game? Or at the very least, not have a negative reaction when someone says, "It's time to play baseball."

There is an intuitive understanding when it comes to sports that intrinsic motivation is paramount to getting better: that skill and affect are inextricably linked. Yet when it comes to reading, this intuitive concept of enjoyment being foundational to improvement seems to go away. The disconnect is that while teachers and administrators understand that motivation is one of the most important ingredients for success in school, the goals we are given through standards and district expectations do not reflect this fundamental concept.

In his book *Readicide*, Kelly Gallagher (2009) argues that, while there may be many factors that contribute to one's reading life and habits, some schools are furthering a decline in reading motivation by assigning difficult texts that not all students can comprehend and valuing test preparation over the goal of creating lifelong readers. The pressure to perform well on state assessments seems to have created curricula that are often geared toward the test, perpetuating the false notion that the way for students to get better at Test A and B is to have in-class activities that mirror Test A and B all year. For too many students, reading in school is being equated with reading grade-level passages, with the only goal to properly fill in the right bubble to answer a comprehension question.

While there are certainly valid arguments for having students practice and be familiar with the very reading tasks they will be assessed on, there starts to be an invisible diminishing return when this preparation, which in no way reflects the reasons people love to read, becomes the main type of reading students experience all year. This is not to say test preparation is not important or that students should not be exposed to grade-level texts and content. Of course they should. What I am arguing is that students will perform better on tests if there is an intentional ratio, so that test preparation is *on top of* a foundation where the tasks (and texts) prioritize both the affective and cognitive aspects of reading, where enjoyment of reading is an explicit goal.

Teachers can also explicitly reinforce connections between the high attention habits of mind emphasized in HART and testing. If students take their state ELA test in May, for example, you can have a 2-week period in late March or early April when students stay in their regular seats but use the HART format to read practice tests, where they get to talk for a few minutes about what the passage was about and any words they didn't know before moving on to the multiple-choice questions. The goal is to encourage the same heightened attention to reading and vocabulary even with this type of text that has no color photographs and was created for a different purpose. Then, as the date of the test gets closer, students can start reading passages and take the practice tests in the same manner as the actual test, completely on their own.

A MATTER OF EQUITY

While the concept of equity is not front and center with HART, it is very much a driver in its design. School classrooms are often designed to favor the motivated student. One might argue this is not intentional. But, as has been discussed several times throughout this book, traditional ways of teaching reading and writing often perpetuate the Matthew effect (Stanovich, 1986) where those who are the more motivated students, often the same students who are higher performing academically, are the ones who can more easily connect with and engage with the teaching.

The best example of this differential experience is the whole-class question-and-answer session where the teacher asks a question and calls on students who have their hands up. The students who raise their hands are more likely to be motivated and academically confident. Since they are the ones who will get called on, they are also the ones who, by answering questions, are actively and not passively engaged with the material: they get to exercise their expressive vocabulary, the active formulation of ideas into words, and, importantly, the positive feedback that often comes afterwards. Meanwhile the less motivated students who tend to be (although are not always) the students who are below grade level or second language learners or less confident students, will at most listen to their peers' answers: they do not use their vocabulary or engage in active thinking or experience the feedback that follows.

This snowball effect of confidence and practice has nothing to do with teachers' caring for their students. Teachers who genuinely care for and believe in all of their students, of course, matter a great deal. But unless that caring is coupled with instruction that looks at the internal cognitive and affective experience of instruction across all 25 students, there will still be a Matthew effect running quietly underneath the school year. This is not to say that we should not have times where there are whole-class conversations. The public sharing of ideas is an important aspect of synthesizing learning as a class. What matters is what is occurring *in addition* to whole-class conversations. Having even just 2 minutes for all students to turn-and-talk before a whole-class conversation, for example, invites every single person in a classroom to actively partake in the work of thinking. Like the simple act of a turn and talk, HART is based on the idea that it is not just what is said in the classroom that matters but also who gets to say it.

The other reason equity is at the heart of HART is that it targets literacy skills that, while important for all students, have seen disparities among students of different socioeconomic and ethnic backgrounds. Differences in proficiency with informational text and background knowledge matter, not just for content learning, but for reading comprehension; prior content knowledge is known to be a strong predictor of reading performance (Cervetti & Wright, 2020). Socioeconomic differences also contribute to gaps in young children's content knowledge in ways that go beyond differences in school and reading (Neuman, 2006). High-income families, for example, tend to have access to more out-of-school experiences such as paid after-school programs, summer camps, and even international vacations, all of which contribute to development of background knowledge (Alexander et al., 2007). Throwing in the twice-a-week science or social studies lesson in the elementary grades is not enough. Finding ways to equal this playing field of background knowledge early on through wide reading of informational text is critical if we are to truly see schools as the great equalizer they were intended to be.

Inequities also often exist in the types of discourse students get to do in school. Although there are plenty of examples that break with this rule, there tends to be far more student-centered talk in high-income schools compared to low-income schools, which are more likely to rely on highly scripted reading programs and have far more teacher-directed discourse (Diamond, 2007; Duke, 2000). Such discrepancies require both schools and teachers to be reflective since it is the less explicit biases—decisions made about who is ready or capable for certain types of discourse—that are more likely to persist unnoticed in classrooms today as opposed to more outward and unequivocal explicit biases.

A final, but rarely highlighted point about instruction that relates to informational text, especially the independent reading of this genre, is that the concept of developing students who are more engaged, careful readers of nonfiction is not just a matter of academic achievement. The ability and decision to read informational text can affect what kind of citizens we become in society, a concept that is especially true in today's information-rich world (Li et al., 2018). Few educators would disagree that we want to send our children out into the world as curious, lifelong readers and that this is an important goal of any education system. But what are we doing to make that happen? The only place I have seen "foster a love of reading" in standards has been in those related to library media. But shouldn't concepts such as curiosity or a love of reading be a key part of the standards in English Language Arts or in any content subject for that matter?

In the meantime, as most teachers know, putting a priority on attending to the affective side of learning is up to us—those of us who are in the schools with children every day who, like all of us, are absolutely bound by the human condition and the complex but very real relationship between motivation, engagement, and learning. The work is never easy. But the more we can create space in the classroom for all students to feel capable and curious with informational texts, the more we can get students to engage not just their mind but also their heart.

HART Lessons

LESSON 1: HART INTRODUCTION

Lesson Goal: Students understand the purpose of HART and the different steps they will learn in the upcoming lessons.

Materials: Anchor chart with HART steps, list of student groups

Lesson Introduction: Narrative Versus Informational Text	Using a Venn Diagram on the board or screen, have students talk about differences between fiction and nonfiction books. You can include turn and talk, interactive writing, and/or whole-class discussion.
	After students have shared what they know, highlight the differences in how much effort and attention each genre requires to comprehend and why. You can also discuss why it's important to get good at reading informational text (how the amount and expectations for reading the genre increases, especially between elementary and middle school).
Introduction of HART	Introduce HART by explaining what each letter stands for, that it is designed to help us get better at reading informational text, and explain when during the week they will be doing HART.
	Pointing to an anchor chart of the steps in HART, briefly describe each step that will occur every time you do HART.
HART Spots	Let students know who is in which HART team and where each team will meet. A visual on a slide can be helpful for this step.
	Explain expectations for transitioning into HART spots, including the signal for moving, how long it should take, and what materials they will eventually bring. Before moving, you can have students turn and talk or point to where they will be going.
	Have students practice getting into HART teams at least twice.
Lesson Wrap-Up	Let students know when they will do the next HART lesson, which is about choosing and recording books. If students are using HART folders, they could decorate them at this point.

LESSON 2: CHOOSING BOOKS

Lesson Goal: Students learn how to choose books from the library and record their choices.

Materials needed: Student folders with book checklists inside, a model folder with a colored sticker, pencils, labeled HART bins

HART Library Introduction	Review the categories of books that are in the HART library. If you are using a book checklist, you can also give students a copy at this point.
	Explain how students will know what book they can choose, reiterating the importance of reading books on their level. If you are using color-coded dots, demonstrate where on the book they can find them. Each group should already know their assigned color.
Choosing Books	Model expectations for choosing sets of books such as one person from a team choosing at a time, where to put the rubber bands, and how to fill out their book checklist.
	Have students get into their HART teams, giving feedback on their transition and practicing again if needed. If students are using a book checklist, they should bring their folder with them. Once seated, have one person from each team choose a set of books. Check to make sure teams are choosing books that match their assigned color.
Recording Books	Once all students have chosen books, you can model how to fill out the book checklist and then have students fill out their own forms. You can also at this time review expectations for what students should do when they need to choose a new book.
	After all teams have recorded their book choice, have each team share out with the class what book they chose.
Putting Away Materials	Explain to students where and how HART books and folders will be put away each time (HART bins, cubbies, desks, etc.), modeling this step if needed. Dismiss teams, reminding them to put their materials back in the correct place.
Lesson Wrap-Up	Tell students that in the next lesson they will start the first step of HART, which is called "What Do You Know?"

LESSON 3: WHAT DO YOU KNOW & WORD QUIZ INTRODUCTION

Lesson Goal: Students learn how to do the What Do You Know? and Word Quiz steps in HART.

Materials: HART bins with students' folders and chosen texts

Lesson Introduction: Background Knowledge	Draw students' attention back to an anchor chart (or slide) that shows the steps of HART and remind them that in today's lesson they will learn the first two steps, the first one being What Do You Know? Let them know today they will practice these steps as a class and then do them in their HART teams in the next lesson.
	Discuss as a class what background knowledge means and/or why teachers ask students to talk about what they already know before a read aloud or shared reading.
	Review that we have different levels of background knowledge: sometimes we know a lot of about a subject and sometimes concepts are familiar or we know we learned about them but can't recall specific facts.
What Do You Know? Practice	Explain that in What Do You Know? students will be doing a similar task, talking about what they already know about a topic, either by looking at the cover if the book is new or remembering what they read the last time, except they will be the ones driving the conversation. Remind students they can ask each other "What do you know about . . .?" or "What do you remember about . . .?"
	Model with the cover of an informational text and ask for a few students to offer their own background knowledge. Remind students they can use any visual on the cover to think about information they know. Then show a cover of a different book. Have students practice initiating this step at their desks by asking each other "What do you know about . . .?"
	Debrief by asking students how the conversation went. What did they talk about? How did the discussion get initiated?

(*Continued*)

Word Quiz Practice	Direct students back to the HART anchor chart and the Word Quiz step. Ask students how words are different in informational books compared to stories. Explain that in Word Quiz they will have time to talk about the vocabulary words in their books for a few minutes before they start reading.
	Hand out charts students can keep in their folder that show the three types of Word Quizzes: Glossary Word Quiz, Word List Quiz, and Word Search (see Appendix C) and review each type. To scaffold understanding, practice with three different types of text as a class using either handouts or examples on the screen. For handouts you would need one page that shows a Glossary, one page with a Word List and one page that has text with bolded words.
	Remind students to use ask the question "What do you know about the word . . .?" and that it is not about getting a definition right or wrong but sharing anything you know about a word. As students practice each type of Word Quiz, walk around and give feedback as needed. After each practice, you can debrief as a class and ask students to share what they knew about different words.
Lesson Wrap-Up and Review	After students put away their Word Quiz sheet in their folders, remind them they can use it when they do HART on their own.
	Review the two steps students learned today by asking students to turn and talk. Suggested prompts are, "What do you ask each other to start What Do You Know?" and "See you if you can tell each other the three types of Word Quizzes and how they are different without looking in your folder."

LESSON 4: WHAT DO YOU KNOW & WORD QUIZ PRACTICE

Lesson Goal: Students practice the first two steps of HART in their teams.

Materials needed: HART bins with students' folders and chosen texts

Lesson Introduction	Remind students of the first two steps they practiced as a class, What Do You Know? and Word Quiz; then let them know that today they will be doing these steps with their own books in their HART teams. Before giving the transition signal, also remind students to bring their books and folders with them.
What Do You Know? Practice	Direct students to do What Do You Know? with their books. Remind students this is not about predicting what the book will be about but talking about anything they know about the topic. Remind them they can use the visuals on the cover for ideas of what to talk about.
	Debrief how this part went. Ask several teams to describe their conversation.
Word Quiz Practice	Tell students to take out their Word Quiz charts and to discuss which Word Quiz makes sense to do based on the type of book they have. You can debrief students' choices or just indicate that once they decide, they can go ahead and do the Word Quiz. Remind students to use the question "What do you know about the word . . .?" As students do the Word Quiz, walk around and listen in, giving positive or suggestive feedback.
	Debrief how this part went. Ask several teams to describe their conversation and what type of Word Quiz they used.
Lesson Wrap-Up	Direct students' attention back to the Word Quiz anchor chart. Let them know the next time they do HART they will be adding on the main part, which is when they start reading the book and talking about what they learned.

LESSON 5: READ AND SHARE

Lesson Goal: Students practice the Read and Share step of HART.

Materials needed: HART bins with students' folders and chosen texts

Lesson Introduction	Remind students that since they already did What Do You Know? and Word Quiz in the last lesson, when they get in their teams they will move on to the Read and Share.
	Have students get in their HART teams with their materials and then look up when they are ready.
Read and Share Directions	Explain to students how the Read and Share portion of HART will be run and that all the reading they do in HART is independent: this is not a time to read aloud to each other. Also important is emphasizing that good readers take their time, fast reading does not make you a better reader.
	Let students know how many minutes they have to read and the signal for when they know to stop and then talk with each other about what they learned.
	You can also remind students at this point that the goal is quality reading—getting good at reading with a high degree of attention and that once you see students are reading well, you might increase the number of minutes they read at a time.
Read and Share Practice #1	Give the signal to begin reading silently. Monitor students as they read and start again if many students are off task. Once the timer goes off, remind students it's time to talk in their teams about one thing they each learned or thought was interesting. Let students know that the goal is keep talking about what they learned until it's time to read again.
Read and Share Practice #2	Give the signal to begin reading silently, again monitoring as they read. Once the timer goes off, remind students to talk in their teams about one or more things they learned or thought were interesting.
	If time permits, practice the Read and Share a third time.
Lesson Wrap-Up	As a class, debrief how this part of HART went. What were some things students shared when they were talking? Was there anything that went well? Were there any challenges?

LESSON 6: HART: DOING IT ON YOUR OWN

Lesson Goal: Students do all of the HART steps.

Materials needed: HART bins with students' folders and chosen texts

Lesson Introduction	Let students know that today they will be doing all the HART steps together: What Do You Know?, Word Quiz, and then the Read and Share. Emphasize that every time they do HART, whether they are starting a new book or are continuing with a book from last time, they do all three steps. For additional scaffolding you can have a turn and talk in which students see if they can name each step and explain what it is.
	Before students get into teams, remind them that even though you, the teacher, will be facilitating when to start each step, the students are in charge of starting and facilitating the conversations.
What Do You Know?	After students get into teams, give the signal or timer to start What Do You Know? and then walk around to monitor and listen in. When the timer is up, announce it is time to move on to Word Quiz.
Word Quiz	Walk around to monitor and listen in on the Word Quiz. When the timer is up, announce it is time to move on to Read and Share.
Read and Share	Using the timer, facilitate movement between silent reading and times to talk. In the beginning the teacher role is mainly facilitator. As students become more independent you can transition to supporting students through individual and group conferences.
	Students should do at least two or three iterations of the Read and Share.
Lesson Wrap-Up	After students put away materials and come back to their desks, debrief how HART went today. Then let them know that next time they do HART, they will get their reader's notebooks.
	If students seem to need more practice, you can do HART several more times before moving on to the next lesson when notebooks are introduced.

LESSON 7: HART NOTEBOOKS

Lesson Goal: Students learn expectations for writing after reading.

Materials needed: HART bins with students' folders and chosen texts, HART notebooks, sharpened pencils

Lesson Introduction	Give students feedback on how they did doing all the steps of HART for the first time. Explain that now, each time after the Read and Share, they will write about what they learned and what they think about that information.
HART	Facilitate all three steps of HART with a timer. Students should do at least two or three sessions of Read and Share before moving on to writing.
Reader's Notebooks	Explain expectations for writing in reader's notebooks including: how much time they will have to write each time, that they can write about both what they learned *and* what they think about that information, and that they will have time to share what they wrote at the end.
	Put the timer on and remind students they can think about what came up in their Read and Share conversations if they are stuck about what to write. As students write, walk around and monitor, giving feedback where appropriate.
Reader's Notebook Share	When the timer goes off, tell students they can share what they wrote in their teams for several minutes. Then you can choose two students to share out loud with the class.
	Dismiss HART teams. Everyone should put away their materials except the two students who will share with the class.

To further support autonomy, you can have students fill out the "Do You Have HART?" shown in Figure 5.6 in Chapter 5. A blank copiable is also available in Appendix C.

Once students understand the steps in HART and expectations for writing in reader's notebooks, the teachers' role shifts from teaching students how to do HART to supporting and lifting up their reading, writing, and discussions through monitoring, group conferences, individual conferences, and minilessons.

Lessons for Student-Facilitated HART

The following are two additional lessons for teachers who want students to move through HART at their own pace.

INDEPENDENCE LESSON 1

Lesson Goal: Students do the What Do You Know? and Word Quiz steps on their own and practice the Read and Share portion on their own.

Materials: Anchor chart with HART steps, student timers (if using them)

Lesson Introduction	Review the steps of HART students have learned in the last few weeks and explain that today they will start practicing doing these steps on their own. You can also explain the benefits of students running HART on their own but also emphasize the importance of keeping voices to a certain level.
Practicing What Do You Know? and Word Quiz	Explain that for today rather than doing all the steps on their own, they are going to practice transitioning from What Do You Know? to the Word Quiz on their own. You can offer suggestions for about how many minutes they might want to give for each step. Or, if timers are used, expectations around using them should be introduced at this time. If students are not using timers, remind them it is up to them when to move on from What Do You Know? to Word Quiz.
	Once time is up, have a class debrief about how this part of being independent went. How did they move from one part to the next? How was it using the timers?

(Continued)

Read and Share Practice	Have a class discussion about the expectations for the Read and Share portion of HART. If students are using timers, they should know how many minutes to set timers for, both for reading and the talk. If students are not using timers, then have a short lesson on how to decide where to read up to as a team, using text features as stopping places. You can also set the expectation that, since they may finish at slightly different times, they can back and review any diagrams or photographs more closely if they are waiting for teammates to finish.
	After the Read and Share, debrief as a class about how this part went.

INDEPENDENCE LESSON 2

Lesson Goal: Students go through all steps of HART (except reader's notebooks) on their own.

Materials: Anchor chart with HART steps, student timers (if using them)

Lesson Introduction	Offer feedback on how the previous independent lesson went and explain that today they will be totally self-sufficient (either with or without timers) in going through the steps of HART. Review any supports that are available such as the anchor chart or handouts in their folder. Students should also know how many minutes they have overall to do What Do You Know?, Word Quiz, and Read and Share.
	Remind students that after this lesson, there will not be any more teaching about expectations. From then on you will just be able to announce, "It's time for HART!" and they will be independent, which will allow you time to start listening in on groups to give feedback.
HART on Their Own	As students do HART on their own, walk around to give feedback as needed.
	Before moving on to reader's notebooks, you can debrief as a class about how it went running HART on their own.
Reader's Notebooks	Either today or in a subsequent lesson, teach expectations for reader's notebooks as described in Appendix A.

Copiables for **HART**

Name _____

Teacher _____

HART BOOK CHECKLIST

Date	Title of Book	Plants & Animals	Weather & Nature	Space and Planets	Energy & Light	Government	History	World Cultures	Other

STUDENT HANDOUT OF WORD QUIZ OPTIONS

WORD QUIZ OPTIONS

Glossary Word Quiz	Choose 3–4 words from the Glossary to talk about in your team. After your team shares what they know about the word, read the definition.
Word List Quiz	Choose 3–4 words from the list of content vocabulary to talk about in your team.
Word Search	Each person chooses 1 or 2 words from the text to "quiz" the group on.

FORM TO REVIEW HART STEPS

DO YOU HAVE HART?

Name _____ Date _____

	Explain It!	Draw It!	Act It Out!
Filling Out Book List			
What Do You Know?			
Word Quiz			
Read and Share			
Writing in Reader's Notebooks			

HART ASSESSMENT RUBRIC

HART Team _____

	Not Visible	Needs Improvement	Yes, Doing a Good Job!	Notes
Choosing books on your level				
Book list filled out correctly				
Reading a range of topics				
Doing all steps in HART				
Notebooks entries reflect time given				
Notebook entries include information and thinking				

STEPS IN HART JUNIOR FOR PRIMARY GRADES

HART JUNIOR

What Do You Know?

Before reading, ask students to turn and talk about what they know about this topic or, if you are continuing with the same read aloud, what they remember from last time. Then have several students share out with the class.

"I know that . . ."

"I remember that . . ."

Word Quiz

Choose three content vocabulary words from the book (the Glossary, Word List, or text). Words can be from upcoming pages or from pages they already read. For each word, have students turn and talk and ask each other: "What do you know about the word . . .?" before having a class conversation about these words.

"What do you know about the word. . . .?"

Read and Share

Read short segments of the read aloud. After each segment, have students turn to each other and talk about what they learned. Repeat this Read and Share format at least three times. Remind students that they will be able to draw and write what they talked about afterwards. (Once students understand how to do HART Jr., you can start encouraging different types of thinking during the share time.)

Reader's Notebooks or Folders

Students go back to their desks or tables to draw, label, and write about the information they remember from the read aloud and their conversations. At the end, students share what they drew and wrote with each other followed by a whole-class share.

References

Afflerbach, P., Cho, B. Y., & Kim, J. Y. (2015). Conceptualizing and assessing higher-order thinking in reading. *Theory into Practice, 54*(3), 203–212.

Aguiar, O. G., Mortimer, E. F., & Scott, P. (2010). Learning from and responding to students' questions: The authoritative and dialogic tension. *Journal of Research in Science Teaching, 47*(2), 174–193.

Anderson, R. C., & Nagy, W. E. (1993). *The vocabulary conundrum* (Report No. 570). Center for the Study of Reading Technical Report.

August, D., Carlo, M., Dressler, C., & Snow, C. (2005). The critical role of vocabulary development for English language learners. *Learning Disabilities Research & Practice, 20*(1), 50–57.

Avargil, S., Lavi, R., & Dori, Y. J. (2018). Students' metacognition and metacognitive strategies in science education. In Y. J. Dori, R. M. Zemira, & D. R. Baker (Eds.), *Cognition, metacognition, and culture in STEM education* (pp. 33–64). Springer, Cham.

Barone, D., & Barone, R. (2016). "Really," "Not Possible," "I Can't Believe It": Exploring Informational Text in Literature Circles. *The Reading Teacher, 70*(1), 69–81.

Beck, I. L., McKeown, M. G., Hamilton, R. L., & Kugan, L. (1997). *Questioning the author: An approach for enhancing student engagement with text.* Newark, DE: International Reading Association.

Beck, I. L., McKeown, M. G., & Kucan, L. (2013, 2002). *Bringing words to life: Robust vocabulary instruction.* Guilford Press.

Berne, J. C., & Degener, S. C. (2015). *The one-on-one reading and writing conference: Working with students on complex texts.* Teachers College Press.

Best, R., Floyd, R., & McNamara, D. (2008). Differential competencies contributing to children's comprehension of narrative and expository texts. *Reading Psychology, 29*(2), 137–164.

Bishop, R. S. (1990). Mirrors, windows, and sliding glass doors. *Perspectives, 6*(3), ix–xi.

Blachowicz, C. L., Fisher, P. J., Ogle, D., & Watts-Taffe, S. (2006). Vocabulary: Questions from the classroom. *Reading Research Quarterly, 41*(4), 524–539.

Bravo, M. A., Hiebert, E. H., & Pearson, P. D. (2007). Tapping the linguistic resources of Spanish/English bilinguals: The role of cognates in science. In R. Wagner, A. Muse, & K. Tannenbaum (Eds.), *Vocabulary acquisition: Implications for reading comprehension* (pp. 140–156).

Calkins, L. M. (2001). *The art of teaching reading.* Prentice Hall.

Carota, F. Posado, A., Harquel, S. Delpeuch, C., Bertrand, O., & Sirigu, A. (2009). Neural dynamics in the intention to speak. *Cerebral Cortex, 20,* 1891–1897.

Cazden, C. (2001). *Classroom discourse: The language of teaching and learning.* Portsmouth, NH: Heinemann.

Cervetti, G. N., & Wright, T. S. (2020). The role of knowledge in understanding and learning from text. In E. Birr Moje, P. P. Afflerbach, P. Encisco, & N. K. Lequx (Eds.), *Handbook of reading research* (p. 5).

Chalk, K., & Bizo, L. A. (2004). Specific praise improves on-task behavior and numeracy enjoyment: A study of year four pupils engaged in the numeracy hour. *Educational Psychology in Practice, 20*(4), 335–351.

Crosson, A. C., McKeown, M. G., Robbins, K. P., & Brown, K. J. (2019). Key elements of robust vocabulary instruction for emergent bilingual adolescents. *Language, Speech, and Hearing Services in Schools, 50*(4), 493–505.

Cummins, J. (1979). Linguistic interdependence and the educational development of bilingual children. *Review of Educational Research, 49*(2), 222–251.

Daniels, H. (2002). *Literature circles: Voice and choice in book clubs and reading groups.* Stenhouse.

Dewitz, P., Jones, J., & Leahy, S. (2009). Comprehension strategy instruction in core reading programs. *Reading Research Quarterly, 44*(2), 102–126.

Duke, N. K. (2004). The case for informational text. *Educational Leadership, 61*(6), 40–45.

Duke, N. K., Purcell-Gates, V., Hall, L. A., & Tower, C. (2006). Authentic literacy activities for developing comprehension and writing. *The Reading Teacher, 60*(4), 344–355.

Ebe, A. E. (2010). Culturally relevant texts and reading assessment for English language learners. *Reading Horizons: A Journal of Literacy and Language Arts, 50*(3), 5.

Eccles, J. S., Midgley, C., Wigfield, A., Buchanan, C. M., Reuman, D., Flanagan, C., & Mac Iver, D. (1993). Development during adolescence: The impact of stage-environment fit on young adolescents' experiences in schools and in families. *American Psychologist, 48*(2), 90–101.

Evans, M., & Boucher, A. R. (2015). Optimizing the power of choice: Supporting student autonomy to foster motivation and engagement in learning. *Mind, Brain, and Education, 9*(2), 87–91.

Feger, M. V. (2006). "I want to read": How culturally relevant texts increase student engagement in reading. *Multicultural Education, 13*(3), 18–18.

Fisher, D., Frey, N., & Lapp, D. (2016). *Text complexity: Stretching readers with texts and tasks.* Corwin Press.

Fitzgerald, J., Elmore, J., Kung, M., & Stenner, A. J. (2017). The conceptual complexity of vocabulary in elementary-grades core science program textbooks. *Reading Research Quarterly, 52*(4), 417–442.

Franklin, K. (2010). Thank you for sharing: Developing students' social skills to improve peer writing conferences. *English Journal, 99*(5), 79–84.

Gallagher, K. (2009). *Readicide: How schools are killing reading and what you can do about it.* Stenhouse Publishers.

Gambrell, L. B. (1996). Creating classroom cultures that foster reading motivation. *Reading Teacher, 50,* 14–25.

Gardner, D. (2004). Vocabulary input through extensive reading: A comparison of words in children's narrative and expository reading materials. *Applied Linguistics, 25*(1), 1–37.

Goodrich, J. M., Lonigan, C. J., & Farver, J. M. (2013). Do early literacy skills in children's first language promote development of skills in their second language? An experimental evaluation of transfer. *Journal of Educational Psychology, 105*(2), 414.

Graesser, A. C., McNamara, D. S., & Louwerse, M. M. (2003). What do readers need to learn in order to process coherence relations in narrative and expository text. In A. P. Sweet, & C. E. Snow (Eds.), *Rethinking reading comprehension* (pp. 82–98). Guilford Press.

Graham, S., & Hebert, M. (2011). Writing to read: A meta-analysis of the impact of writing and writing instruction on reading. *Harvard Educational Review, 81*(4), 710–744.

Graves, M. F. (2016). *The vocabulary book: Learning and instruction.* Teachers College Press.

Graves, M. F., August, D., & Mancilla-Martinez, J. (2012). *Teaching vocabulary to English language learners.* Teachers College Press.

Graves, M. F., & Watts-Taffe, S. (2008). For the love of words: Fostering word consciousness in young readers. *The Reading Teacher, 62*(3), 185–193.

Guccione, L. (2012). *Oral language development and ELLs: 5 challenges and solutions.* Colorín Colorado.

Guthrie, J. T., & Taboada Barber, A. M. (2011). Best practices in motivating students to read. In L. M. Morrow & L. B. Gambrell (Eds.), *Best practices in literacy instruction* (pp. 177–198). Guilford Press.

Guthrie, J. T., Wigfield, A., Barbosa, P., Perencevich, K. C., Taboada Barber, A., Davis, M. H., Scafiddi, N. T., & Tonks, S. (2004). Increasing reading comprehension and engagement through concept-oriented reading instruction. *Journal Educational of Psychology, 96*(3), 403.

Guthrie, J. T., Wigfield, A., Metsala, J. L., & Cox, K. E. (1999). Motivational and cognitive predictors of text comprehension and reading amount. *Scientific Studies of Reading, 3*(3), 231–256.

Hale, E. (2008). *Crafting writers, K-6.* Stenhouse.

Hale, E. (2014). *Readers writing: Lessons for responding to narrative and informational texts.* Stenhouse.

Hale, E. (2018). Academic praise in conferences: A key for motivating struggling writers. *The Reading Teacher, 71*(6), 651–658.

Hale, E., & Kim, J. S. (2020). Providing platforms: An examination of low-level questions in informational read-alouds. *The Elementary School Journal, 120*(4), 555–579.

Hammond, J., & Gibbons, P. (2005). What is scaffolding. *Teachers' Voices, 8,* 8–16.

Hannah, K. (2015). *The nightingale.* St. Martin's Press.

Harmon, J. M., Hedrick, W. B., & Wood, K. D. (2005). Research on vocabulary instruction in the content areas: Implications for struggling readers. *Reading & Writing Quarterly, 21*(3), 261–280.

Harvey, S., & Goudvis, A. (2007). *Strategies that work: Teaching comprehension for understanding and engagement.* Stenhouse Publishers.

Hebbecker, K., Förster, N., & Souvignier, E. (2019). Reciprocal effects between reading achievement and intrinsic and extrinsic reading motivation. *Scientific Studies of Reading, 23*(5), 419–436.

Herrero, E. A. (2006). Using Dominican oral literature and discourse to support literacy learning among low-achieving students from the Dominican Republic. *International Journal of Bilingual Education and Bilingualism, 9*(2), 219–238.

Hiebert, E. H. (2014). *The forgotten reading proficiency: Stamina in silent reading.* Text Project & University of California, Santa Cruz.

Hirsch, E. (2003). Reading comprehension requires knowledge-of words and the world. *American Educator, 27*(1), 10–13.

Hwang, H., & Duke, N. K. (2020). Content counts and motivation matters: Reading comprehension in third-grade students who are English learners. *AERA Open, 6*(1), 2332858419899075.

Jang, H., Reeve, J., & Deci, E. (2010). Engaging students in learning activities: It is not autonomy support or structure but autonomy support and structure. *Journal of Educational Psychology, 102*(3), 588.

Keats, E. (1962). *The snowy day.* Penguin.

Kelsky, K. (2015). *The professor is in: The essential guide to turning your Ph. D. into a job.* Crown.

Kintsch, W. (1988). The role of knowledge in discourse comprehension: A construction-integration model. *Psychological Review, 95*(2), 163.

Kintsch, W., & Van Dijk, T. A. (1978). Toward a model of text comprehension and production. *Psychological Review, 85*(5), 363.

Leopold, C., & Leutner, D. (2012). Science text comprehension: Drawing, main idea selection, and summarizing as learning strategies. *Learning and Instruction, 22*(1), 16–26.

Li, D., Beecher, C., & Cho, B. Y. (2018). Examining the reading of informational text in 4th grade class and its relation with students' reading performance. *Reading Psychology, 39*(1), 1–28.

Lou, Y., Abrami, P. C., Spence, J. C., Poulsen, C., Chambers, B., & d'Apollonia, S. (1996). Within-class grouping: A meta-analysis. *Review of Educational Research, 66*(4), 423–458.

Maloch, B., & Bomer, R. (2013). Informational texts and the common core standards: What are we talking about, anyway? *Language Arts, 90*(3), 205.

Margolis, H., & McCabe, P. P. (2004). Self-efficacy: A key to improving the motivation of struggling learners. *The Clearing House: A Journal of Educational Strategies, Issues and Ideas, 77*(6), 241–249.

Martin, J. B., & Azarian, M. (1998). *Snowflake Bentley.* Houghton Mifflin Company.

McCauley, J. K., & McCauley, D. S. (1992). Using choral reading to promote language learning for ESL students. *The Reading Teacher, 45*, 526–533.

Michaels, S., & O'Connor, C. (2012). *Talk science primer.* Cambridge, MA: TERC.

Michaels, S., O'Connor, C., & Resnick, L. B. (2008). Deliberative discourse idealized and realized: Accountable talk in the classroom and in civic life. *Studies in Philosophy and Education, 27*(4), 283–297.

Moss, B. (2005). Making a case and a place for effective content area literacy instruction in the elementary grades. *The Reading Teacher, 59*(1), 46–55.

Moss, B. (2015). Getting the picture: Visual dimensions of informational texts. In *Handbook of research on teaching literacy through the communicative and visual arts* (Vol. II, pp. 421–426). Routledge.

Murphy, P. K., Greene, J. A., Firetto, C. M., Li, M., Lobczowski, N. G., Duke, R. F., Wei, L., & Croninger, R. M. (2017). Exploring the influence of homogeneous versus heterogeneous grouping on students' text-based discussions and comprehension. *Contemporary Educational Psychology, 51*, 336–355.

Nagy, W. E., García, G. E., Durgunoğlu, A. Y., & Hancin-Bhatt, B. (1993). Spanish-English bilingual students' use of cognates in English reading. *Journal of Reading Behavior, 25*(3), 241–259.

National Governors Association Center for Best Practices (NGACBP), Council of Chief State School Officers. (2010). *Common Core State Standards.* Washington, DC: National Governors Association Center for Best Practices, Council of Chief State School Officers.

Neuman, S. B., Kaefer, T., & Pinkham, A. (2014). Building background knowledge. *The Reading Teacher, 68*(2), 145–148.

Nicholson, D. M. (2016). *The school the Aztec eagles built.* Lee & Low.

Ogle, D. M. (1986). KWL: A teaching model that develops active reading of expository text. *The Reading Teacher, 39*(6), 564–570.

Palinscar, A. S., & Brown, A. L. (1984). Reciprocal teaching of comprehension-fostering and comprehension-monitoring activities. *Cognition and Instruction, 1*(2), 117–175.

Pearson, P. D., & Gallagher, M. C. (1983). The instruction of reading comprehension. *Contemporary Educational Psychology, 8*(3), 317–344.

Pressley, M. (2001). Effective beginning reading instruction: A paper commissioned by the National Reading Conference. Chicago: National Reading Conference.

Pressley, M., Johnson, C. J., Symons, S., McGoldrick, J. A., & Kurita, J. A. (1989). Strategies that improve children's memory and comprehension of text. *The Elementary School Journal, 90*(1), 3–32.

Rance-Roney, J. A. (2010). Reconceptualizing interactional groups: Grouping schemes for maximizing language learning. In *English teaching forum* (Vol. 48, No. 1, pp. 20–26). Washington, DC: US Department of State. Bureau of Educational and Cultural Affairs, Office of English Language Programs.

Reedy, A., & De Carvalho, R. (2021). Children's perspectives on reading, agency and their environment: What can we learn about reading for pleasure from an East London primary school? *Education 3–13, 49*(2), 134–147.

Reeve, J. (2002). Self-determination theory applied to educational settings. *Handbook of Self-Determination Research, 2*, 183–204.

Ruiz, R. (1984). Orientations in language planning. *NABE Journal, 8*(2), 15–34.

Rumelhart, D. (1980). Schemata: The building blocks of cognition. In R. J. Spiro, B. C. Bruce, & W. F. Brewer (Eds.), *Theoretical issues in reading comprehension.* Hillsdale, NJ: Erlbaum.

Ryan, R. M., & Deci, E. L. (2000). Self-determination theory and the facilitation of intrinsic motivation, social development, and well-being. *American Psychologist, 55*(1), 68.

Santoro, L. E., Baker, S. K., Fien, H., Smith, J. L. M., & Chard, D. J. (2016). Using read-alouds to help struggling readers access and comprehend complex, informational text. *Teaching Exceptional Children, 48*(6), 282–292.

Schleppegrell, M. J. (2012). Academic language in teaching and learning: Introduction to the special issue. *The Elementary School Journal, 112*(3), 409–418.

Shaw, G. (2016). *Curious about snow.* Grosset & Dunlap.

Simonsen, B., Myers, D., & DeLuca, C. (2010). Teaching teachers to use prompts, opportunities to respond, and specific praise. *Teacher Education and Special Education, 33*(4), 300–318.

Snow, C. (2002). *Reading for understanding: Toward an R&D program in reading comprehension.* Rand Corporation.

Snow, C. E., & Uccelli, P. (2009). The challenge of academic language. *The Cambridge Handbook of Literacy, 112,* 133.

Stanovich, K. (1986). Matthew effects in reading: Some consequences of individual differences in the acquisition of literacy. *Reading Research Quarterly, 21*(4), 360–407.

Stone, C. A. (1998). The metaphor of scaffolding: Its utility for the field of learning disabilities. *Journal of Learning Disabilities, 31*(4), 344–364.

Stuart, D., & Volk, D. (2002). Collaboration in a culturally responsive literacy pedagogy: Educating teachers and Latino children. *Reading, 36*(3), 127–134.

Toste, J. R., Didion, L., Peng, P., Filderman, M. J., & McClelland, A. M. (2020). A meta-analytic review of the relations between motivation and reading achievement for K–12 students. *Review of Educational Research, 90*(3), 420–456.

Ushioda, E. (2011). Why autonomy? Insights from motivation theory and research. *Innovation in Language Learning and Teaching, 5*(2), 221–232.

Vasilyeva, M., & Waterfall, H. (2011). Variability in language development: Relation to socioeconomic status and environmental input. In S. Neuman & D. Dickinson (Eds.), *Handbook of early literacy research* (Vol. 3, pp. 36–48). New York: Guildford Press.

Vygotsky, L. S. (1978). *Mind in society.* Harvard University Press.

Wang, J. H. Y., & Guthrie, J. T. (2004). Modeling the effects of intrinsic motivation, extrinsic motivation, amount of reading, and past reading achievement on text comprehension between US and Chinese students. *Reading Research Quarterly, 39*(2), 162–186.

Williams, L. M., Hedrick, W. B., & Tuschlnski, L. (2008). Motivation: Going beyond testing to a lifetime of reading. *Childhood Education, 84*(3), 135–141.

Wood, D., Bruner, J. S., & Ross, G. (1976). The role of tutoring in problem solving. *The Journal of Child Psychology and Psychiatry, 17*(2), 89–100.

Yopp, R. H., & Yopp, H. K. (2012). Young children's limited and narrow exposure to informational text. *The Reading Teacher, 65*(7), 480–490.

Index

About the Author

Elizabeth Hale is an assistant professor of literacy at the University of North Florida's College of Education and Human Services. Her research focuses on supporting engagement with and comprehension of informational texts at the elementary and middle school level and using writing to deepen students' critical thinking about texts. Elizabeth received her EdD from the Harvard Graduate School of Education and her MA from Teachers College at Columbia University. She previously worked for nine years as a teacher and literacy coach in the Boston Public Schools and as an instructor of literacy at Emmanuel College. Elizabeth is the author of _Crafting Writers, K-6_ (Stenhouse, 2008) and _Readers Writing: Lessons for Responding to Narrative and Informational Text_ (Stenhouse, 2014).